Therapy Quest

*An Interactive Journey
through Acceptance and Commitment Therapy*

Janina Scarlet, PhD

ROBINSON

ROBINSON

First published in Great Britain in 2018 by Robinson

Copyright © Janina Scarlet, 2018

1 3 5 7 9 10 8 6 4 2

A CIP catalogue record for this book is available from the British Library

ISBN: 978-1-47213-968-9

Typeset in Adobe Garamond by Hewer Text UK Ltd, Edinburgh
Printed and bound by CPI Group (UK) Ltd, Croydon, CR0 4YY

Papers used by Robinson are from well-managed
forests and other responsible sources

Robinson
An imprint of
Little, Brown Book Group
Carmelite House
50 Victoria Embankment
London EC4Y 0DZ

An Hachette UK Company
www.hachette.co.uk

www.littlebrown.co.uk

To Andrew McAleer for his magical vision.
To Alan, Jay, Travis, Matt and Shannon for all their support.
To Dustin McGinnis for always being right Here, in my heart.

Instructions:
READ AT YOUR OWN RISK

This is an interactive book where you become a character in a psychological quest through a magical world. This quest requires you to make decisions along the way about how to proceed with your mission. Like many role-playing games (RPGs), you will have opportunities to earn or lose points along the way.

The points you earn are broken up into three categories defining your character's basic qualities. You start out with 10 free points, which you can divide in any way you choose between the categories. I recommend that you keep tallying your points throughout the book.

The three character quality categories are:

Courage **Wisdom** **Inner Strength**

You need a total of 50 points to face your main challenge at the end of your quest. Psychologically adaptive decisions earn points in these categories while maladaptive decisions may result in lost points (your points total can even be a negative value in a category if an action forces you to drop below zero points) or your quest being blocked, forcing you to regress to an earlier point. Lose all your points and you'll have to backtrack or just start over. Some choices can even cause your character's death, so be careful!

In this story, you will discover how to use and apply various magical spells, charms and potions based on research-supported psychology therapies, primarily from Acceptance and Commitment Therapy

(ACT) and self-compassion interventions. These skills are intended to help you learn to better cope with your internal monsters, be they dragons of anxiety or your demons of depression.

I wish you a healing and magical journey.

It was the Tuesday before the end of the world. Although, to be honest, it started out as a perfectly boring Tuesday.

Until THEY showed up . . .

You yawn repeatedly as the sound of the rain gently taps on the glass of your window. The alarm clock goes off for the sixth time, and you turn it off with a groan.

One tired foot on the floor and then another. You stayed up until 3 a.m. last night, replaying yesterday's conversation with your friend, Lisa, in your head. You had asked her how she felt about your presentation, and she paused for a moment, forming a letter 'O' with her mouth before replying, 'Oh, you were fine.'

Fine? What in the world did *that* mean? OK, sure, you stumbled a few times, but that doesn't mean your presentation sucked. Or did it?

It did! You know it did.

The more you thought about it, the worse the presentation seemed to you in retrospect. After all, Lisa yawned not once but two times during it, and your friend Matt checked his watch several times. And you didn't answer that one question exactly as you'd wanted to, as you know you should have.

Yep. You completely messed it up. Like you always do . . .

You yawn once more. This isn't the first time you were up all night because your mind insisted on pointing out all the things you did wrong the day, the week, the year before.

You stand up. Then, as thoughts about the presentation return to your mind, some habitual sensations settle in: your heart starts beating fast; your hands and neck are sweating. You've been through this before. Sometimes people tell you to calm down, to get over it, as if you are doing this by choice. They don't understand the loss of control that happens when your emotions become too strong. They don't understand what it's like to try to appear functional while you're battling your demons every single day. You sigh and get ready for another fight, looking for ways to distract yourself until it passes, but this time the familiar feeling of doom is somehow stronger. It feels . . . darker.

You take in a breath, hoping to calm down, only to then suddenly and violently cough. It feels as if you're breathing ash. Chills spread all over your body. Your vision blurs. Something's really wrong this time. Your stomach's sick, as if you've just got off the world's fastest roller coaster.

Is this the day you actually lose your mind? Your life?

Is this a heart attack?

You reach for your phone to call an ambulance but it blocks you with a message announcing, almost with a sneer, that it's in the middle of an update. When it restarts moments later, your passcode is not recognised. Several attempts later you are locked out of your phone. Shaking and breathing heavily, you try to call for help but no sound comes out. You can't even swear.

There is a hiss above your bed. It's dark, but it looks like there's a small hole in the ceiling. And something is seeping through it. Oil? No . . . a dark, thick mist.

You watch, holding your breath in horror, as the mist forms into a shape of a dark skeleton enveloped in black smoke.

You try to shout, 'What are you?' but your voice still won't come.

The mist creature circles around you, engulfing you in its darkness as it hisses, sounding as if the words are projected directly into your brain: 'I KNOW YOU. I SEE YOU. YOU ARE A FAILURE. A LOSER.'

The words feel like cold hands pressing against your head, squeezing your mind. You close your eyes but the monster appears to be even bigger in your mind now. You open your eyes again, see the monster is still there, and sprint out of the room. You race down the hallway and toward the front door, only to see a second mist monster already there, blocking your exit. You quickly turn into the kitchen, hearing the two dark mist creatures hiss as they chase after you.

3

Quickly, you grab a knife from the counter, the largest one you can find. The creatures loom over you and, acting on instinct, you stab them with two quick motions, one and then the other.

The creatures stop their hissing and dissolve on to the floor, the mist now replaced by twin piles of ash. You sigh and lean against the counter in relief. What were those things?

The ashes move and whirl around, and there's that hissing noise again. You curse under your breath as now, instead of two, four mist creatures rise before you. As a chorus, they all loudly hiss into your mind: 'NOBODY LOVES YOU. NOBODY WILL EVER LOVE YOU. YOU WILL DIE ALONE. YOU ARE A FAILURE. YOU ARE A LOSER.'

You hack and slash and jab and stab. Once more, the creatures lose their forms and fall as ash, only to rise again moments later. Once more they've doubled, their voices louder and louder, their words hitting your body harder than before. Your heart is heavy. Your stomach feels as if it's been repeatedly kicked. You're surrounded and desperately make another series of attacks, earning moments of short-term relief before the monsters multiply and grow even louder, their voices causing the dark thoughts to encircle you. After forcing them to become ash again, you kneel on the floor, exhausted, and quickly consider your options.

When you try to run, they block you or follow you. Destroy them and they multiply. But they haven't actually attacked, even when they've had you surrounded. Maybe . . . Maybe all they have is words and mist. If you stand up to them, maybe they won't attack and you can find another option? Or maybe they're teasing and will kill you the moment you let your guard down?

If you choose to face the monsters, go to page 89.

If you choose to keep stabbing these monsters, go to page 51.

Face It

Gain 3 wisdom points

You chose wisely. Avoiding looking at the table is likely to make you more upset and disgusted. Instead, we can look at the table with the eyes of a scientist, or a detective, or perhaps an artist, or a writer. Someone who has to study the table in great detail, full of curiosity and wonder about the table and its contents.

Instead of judging the scenery as disgusting, we can look at it for what it is – a table with insects. Some of the insects are brown; some are black or red. Some are larger and some are smaller than others.

Try focusing on nothing but the image of the table and its contents, observing every detail so carefully that you could draw them. Take two minutes to really study the details of the table.

Ready? Go!

. . .

What did you notice? Chances are that if you did this task, you noticed that over time the images became less distressing and less repulsive.

When faced with anxiety-provoking or distressing images, try observing them this way – without judging them as terrible or repulsive, without turning away. Take a breath and watch, listen and pay attention. The more you're willing to experience what is happening, the less distressing it will likely be.

Continue to page 70.

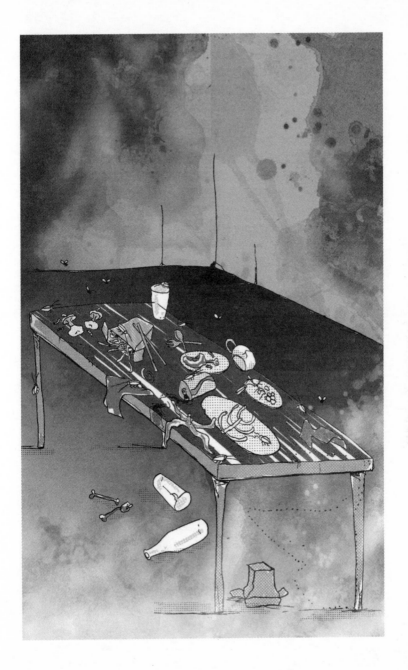

Vulnerability Spell

Gain 4 inner strength points

One of the most magical, though hardest, spells is the Vulnerability Spell. *Vulnerability* is the willingness to be authentic with yourself and others. The Vulnerability Spell might feel bittersweet because you are opening yourself up to others, taking the chance with a possibility that you might get hurt. For example, telling someone that you love them is a vulnerable action. It involves taking a chance, risking rejection and hurt, because the possibility of love and connection is THAT important.

Although people who drink the vulnerability spell are more likely to get hurt compared to people who are unwilling to share themselves with others, they might also experience more love and happiness. Brené Brown, a magical researcher and storyteller, has called these people *wholehearted*. Using the Vulnerability Spell might not be easy but it does seem necessary in order to have meaningful relationships with yourself and others.

Well done!

Turn to page 76 to continue.

Your Quest Begins!

Gain 4 courage points

Congratulations! You have elected to begin your magical quest. Along the way you might face dark spells of insecurity and the pits of vulnerability. But you will also learn healing spells and obtain new potions to help you fight against dark magic.

Are you ready? Proceed to page 137.

You purse your lips as Michael curses out loud.

Hoffman shouts again, 'Put your hands up and surrender yourselves!'

Lex reaches for an arrow, but Hoffman reaches for his club at the same time. Lex curses and puts the arrow back in the quiver.

'Put all your weapons on the ground and surrender yourselves,' Hoffman repeats.

No one moves.

'All right, that's it,' a tall Minotaur says. 'I'm going to count to three. If the weapons don't start dropping, we start clubbing you all, starting with the ugly one.' He points to Gherk. You recognise this Minotaur as Tyreck, Hoffman's boss.

You clench your fists, feeling the tension around you skyrocket. Lex is the first to put down the bow and arrow. Michael grunts before dropping his machete.

'You, fugly one!' Tyreck shouts to Gherk. 'I know you have knives in there. Drop 'em.'

'Hey, you can't talk to him like that!' Michael snaps.

Gherk puts his enormous hand on Michael's shoulder. 'It's, uh, OK, Michael,' he says.

The two men look at one another and take a breath at the same time, with a profound sense of support and understanding. They both nod at one another and Gherk takes out four cooking knives from his apron.

'You too, Lyke!' Tyreck smirks at Blake. 'I know you've got something in that disgusting suit of yours.'

Your shoulders tense even more, you feel your eyebrows narrowing. You want to shout at this indignant brute but you know that it will not do any good.

'I have nothing,' Blake says, looking to the ground.

'I think some friends of yours might disagree,' Tyreck says. He then turns to Hoffman. 'Get the exterminators.'

Hoffman looks back at him. 'Exterminators, sir?'

'Yes, Hoffman! Exterminators! Why do I always have to do everything around here? Get them! Now!'

'Yes, sir.' Hoffman nods and turns to the rest of the SAMs. 'Make way for the exterminators.' He briskly walks through the parting Minotaurs and whistles.

The ground begins to vibrate and tremble with the sound of hundreds of tiny feet stomping on it. You and the rest of the legion members exchange panicked glances.

Hektor and Hera hiss at Tyreck and arch their backs. Tyreck threatens them with his club. 'You'd better calm those animals before I let their skulls meet my trusted club.'

Katrina's eyes well up with tears and her fists tighten. She takes a breath and turns toward the dragopurrs, her voice shaking. 'Hektor. Hera. Down.'

The dragopurrs slowly lie down on the ground and look up at her with their big, sad eyes.

The ground is still shaking and, through the opening crack between the Minotaurs, you can see tiny red figures fast approaching.

Tyreck gives Blake a vicious smile. 'Here they come.'

As the creatures get closer, you see that these are short little imps, each pale-skinned, wearing white trousers and cardigans and tall, pointy red hats.

'Redcaps,' says Blake.

'Welcome, Covetyl,' Tyreck says to the biggest imp wearing the tallest hat. 'We have a surprise for you.' He points to Blake with his club. 'He claims he's clean but will need to be searched.'

'Gladly.' Covetyl grins a nasty smile, revealing his yellowish-black teeth, as he walks around Blake, almost as if checking out a

11

cow for purchase. The imp's eyes are gleaming with malice. He then turns to the rest of his imps. 'All right, boys. This is for all our brothers and sisters who were brutally killed by these filthy Lykes. Our caps are painted with their blood and we won't stop until every single one of them has bled out. We will not stop until all our hats are uniformly red with their grimy blood.' He then turns toward Blake. 'Now, let's see what this one is made of. Let's shake him out.'

At least three dozen imps run up to Blake. They lift him up and turn him upside down, turning his pockets inside out, pinching and biting him. A pair of little pink gloves falls out of his pocket and on to the ground. Blake screams in agony, his eyes flashing red, but he holds himself back from turning.

'Let him down,' Covetyl orders, and the imps drop Blake on the cold cement. 'What's this?' Covetyl asks, picking up Blake's pink gloves with one hand and pulling up Blake's head by his hair with another.

'My winter gloves,' Blake says, his left eyebrow bleeding.

'Disgusting, just like you,' Covetyl says, dropping the gloves back on the ground and smashing Blake's head against the cement.

Blake groans and lifts his head again. His left eye is swollen and his nose is bleeding. The imps are grinning their grotesque yellow teeth at him.

Covetyl then turns to the imps still standing among the Minotaurs. 'My brothers and sisters. This is a clear win for us. Our friendship with the Minotaurs has indeed been proven to be fruitful. Now, Whitecaps, come forward.'

Thirteen imps wearing white caps step forward. Two of them look like children, their caps looking more like giant white hoods, as opposed to hats.

Covetyl addresses them. 'You know the rules. Whoever gets a silver stab in the werewolf gets to wash their hats in his blood – but only the stabs made while he is still conscious enough to feel the pain count.'

'Wait,' Hoffman says to Covetyl and then turns to Tyreck. 'Sir, with all due respect, Mallena's orders were—'

'I know what Mallena's orders were, Sergeant. But don't for a second forget your place here. Don't for a second forget who's in charge of you.'

'But, sir—'

'Shut it, Hoffman!' Tyreck hisses, and then speaks quietly so that you can barely hear what he is saying. 'This alliance with the imps is a very important political move. Don't mess this up.' He then turns to the imps. 'So sorry for this interruption. He's . . . new. He'll get a talking-to, don't you worry. Please, proceed.'

The Whitecaps whip out their silver daggers and step toward Blake.

'Stop!' you shout, and stand between them and the groaning lycanthrope.

The Whitecaps stop, hissing and growling at you.

'And who is this?' Covetyl asks Tyreck.

Tyreck shrugs and turns to Hoffman. 'Who is this?'

'This is the Chosen One, sir.'

Tyreck's eyes widen. He approaches you, towering over you like a gigantic shadow of horror. He walks around you, then finally stops in front of you and smirks. 'You? You are the Chosen One?'

You lower your gaze as the imps and the Minotaurs break into an obnoxious laugh. Suddenly, Tyreck grabs you and holds a knife to your chest.

'If anyone moves, or tries to interfere, including any of those filthy flying things,' he points to the dragopurrs, 'your Chosen One will get a dagger through the heart.'

The legion members look at you with horror in their eyes as you feel stupid, guilty and ashamed for being unable to help Blake. All you can do is watch as Tyreck forcefully turns you around, so that you can see what happens to your friend.

You hear Covetyl behind you say, 'Begin.'

The imps surround Blake, their dreary eyes flickering with hateful glee. Blake growls at them, warning them to stay away. A few of them jump back while the rest continue to approach.

'P-please,' you plead. 'Please. Don't.'

The tallest and the biggest of the imps hops toward Blake and makes to stab him. Blake rolls back and jumps to his feet, his eyes flashing red. Blake swipes at them but misses, and one of the imps jumps under his fist, stabbing his thigh.

You scream, as do most of the legion members. Blake growls, his face beginning to extend and become covered with hair. The imp who stabbed him takes this opportunity to wash his hat in Blake's blood. He then grins, a disgusting grimace, places his bloodstained hood back on his head, and turns to leave.

He doesn't get far. Blake, now fully transformed, jumps on top of him, tearing the imp in half.

'Attack!' Covetyl shouts.

The rest of the Whitecaps run toward Blake, teeth and knives bared. One of the imp children stabs Blake in his other leg and then places his head under the blood flow, while still wearing the cap.

Blake, in his werewolf form, shakes from side to side, and then falls down on the ground. The rest of the Whitecaps charge toward him, stabbing him repeatedly, then wash their caps in his blood. The grotesque scene is too painful to watch but it is impossible to look away.

Blake kills two more Whitecaps in his attempts to stand, but the rest of them overpower him, stabbing him until he stops moving. Several of the imps, whose hats remain white, look angry and disappointed. They prod him but it's of no use.

Behind you, you hear sobs coming from your legion members. You are hoarse from screaming and are numb from the atrocity of what you are seeing. Tyreck throws you down to your knees, as Covetyl addresses his subjects.

'Let's drag him off,' the imp says, pointing to Blake's body.

'What do you want with his body?' Tyreck asks him.

'What's it to you?' Covetyl asks with suspicion in his voice.

'Just curious. Didn't mean any offence.'

Covetyl grins, apparently satisfied with the Minotaur's tone. 'We will drag the Lyke scum through the city for public spitting.'

Your stomach tightens in anger and disgust as Covetyl turns back toward his imps. 'All right, drag him out!'

Blake's body, in full transformation, looks gigantic compared to the tiny, vicious imps, who are grabbing and prodding him. He is covered with blood. His eyes look dim and frozen. As big as he is, he looks helpless against the sea of hatred as several dozen Redcaps grab on to him and begin to drag him away.

Fury burns through you and the world appears in a red filter now.

'DROP HIM!' you snarl in a voice that doesn't sound like your own. You look down and notice your hands are covered with canine fur.

Eribelle gasps and the imps stare at you, their eyes widened.

'You didn't tell me your Chosen One is a werewolf,' Covetyl hisses at Tyreck. 'We had a deal. You're supposed to report and register all werewolves with us to be dealt with.'

'I . . . I didn't know,' Tyreck says. His eyes are as wide as the imp's.

'Well, I guess it's our lucky day,' Covetyl says, turning to face you. 'We get two Lykes for the price of one.'

'No,' Tyreck says. 'You can't kill that one.'

Covetyl sharply turns back to him. 'What did you say, *Minotaur?*'

Tyreck gulps, his eyes becoming wider still. He is clearly uncomfortable. 'It's M-M-Mallena. She gave clear orders to bring the Chosen One to her unharmed.'

'I don't care whose orders you're on. We had an agreement. We get all of them. So, unless you want an imp war on your hands, you will let us have that werewolf.'

Tyreck spits on the ground but says nothing.

'I thought so,' says Covetyl, and then turns to his imps and points at you. 'Attack!'

You growl as several dozen imps charge at you, their knives wickedly glinting in the moonlight.

BANG!

There is a giant explosion and the sky lightens as if it is daylight. When the smoke clears, you see Mallena standing near you. Her lips are tightly pursed and her eyebrows furrowed.

'Stop! Get back!' Mallena shouts at the imps.

The creatures growl at her but stop and retreat.

'What were you thinking?' Mallena shouts at Tyreck.

'I am terribly sorry, my lady,' his voice creaks.

'Hey!' Covetyl shouts at her. 'That is our werewolf. It's ours fair and square.'

'Funny,' Mallena responds, her voice firm and forceful, her eyes squinting with fury, 'I don't remember authorising that.'

'We don't need your permission to authorise this transaction.'

'As the leader of Here and Head of the Magic Consulate, I can tell you that you do, in fact, need my permission. And the Chosen One is mine to deal with, not yours.'

'You won't be the leader of Here for too much longer if I have anything to say about it,' Covetyl spits.

'Luckily, you don't,' she snaps back, and then points her hands to the sky.

Thunderous streaks of lightning illuminate the sky, striking from her very fingertips. Mallena manipulates the lightning and then directs it toward the imps.

'AAH!' several imps scream as nearly a dozen of their kind are struck by lightning.

'No, no, please,' Covetyl pleads, backing away slowly. 'Just keep the damned Lyke. I'm . . . sorry. OK? I'm sorry.' For the first time, he looks afraid.

'I suggest you run,' she says.

The imps slowly back away as Mallena explodes the first batch of lightning behind them. Several dozen of them jump, and all take off running, the ground shaking from the stomping of hundreds of little impish feet, many of their hats on fire.

You sigh with relief.

Mallena smirks and turns to face Tyreck. 'How dare you betray me?'

Tyreck gulps and shudders under her wrath. He takes a breath and puts on a fake smile. 'Look, sweetheart. We were trying to negotiate a deal that would benefit us all. I don't think you fully understand the benefits of—'

SMACK!

Mallena slaps him hard across the face. Tyreck whimpers, rubbing his cheek as Mallena hisses, 'Listen to me, Tyreck! You think that just because I am a woman, you can speak to me that way? I am *not* your sweetheart! I am your ruler, and as my subordinate, you are to follow my every command!'

'Yes, ma'am.' He lowers his head.

'Hoffman,' Mallena says.

'Yes, ma'am.' Hoffman bows his head.

'You have been nothing but loyal to me all these years, and when Tyreck and the SAMs have betrayed me, you were the only one who did not. I value loyalty.'

She then turns back to Tyreck. 'Tyreck.'

'Yes?' Tyreck's voice is shaking.

'You are under arrest for treason. Hoffman is the Chief Special Agent of Magic now.'

'Look, sweetheart, can we at least talk about this?' Tyreck pleads.

'Hoffman!' Mallena shouts.

'Yes, ma'am.'

'Punch him.'

'With pleasure, ma'am.' Hoffman smirks and punches Tyreck in the face. Tyreck goes down.

'Sexist pig,' Mallena murmurs under her breath.

She then turns to you, giving you a big, unsettling smile. She approaches you, looking you up and down. As you lower your gaze, you notice that your hands are back to normal and your red filter has gone.

'So,' Mallena says, looking so deeply into your eyes that you feel her gaze penetrating your very soul. 'You are a werewolf.'

'I am not a werewolf,' you say, looking back at her as you notice a thin, grey choker blinking red around her long, pale neck. 'Being a werewolf is something that happens to me, but it is only a small part of who I am. It's an aspect, not what defines me.'

Mallena smiles. 'You are very wise. It looks like you've learned a lot in the few days that you have been Here. I think you and I are going to get along just fine.'

She then turns to Hoffman. 'Please escort all of them out to the library.'

'Yes, ma'am.' He bows. 'And what would you like me to do with the bodies?' He points to Anka and Blake.

'Bring them too,' she says as she gives you another unsettling smile and walks off.

'All right,' Hoffman says to the SAMs, pointing to you and the legion. 'Bring them all in.'

As the SAMs begin to move toward you, two of them grab you. You recognise one of them as Kasper.

'Please don't fight us,' Kasper says to you in a low voice. 'I have no problem with werewolves but the other SAMs Here aren't so . . . open-minded. I really don't want anyone else to get hurt.'

You let them lead you out without a struggle.

Behind you, you hear Michael's voice. 'Hoffman! Hoffman. Please. Think about this. This isn't what we fought for.'

Hoffman walks ahead, passing you, visibly ignoring Michael's pleas.

'Hoffman, wait,' Lex's voice sounds behind you.

Hoffman stops, sighs and turns around. Two other SAMs drag Lex toward Hoffman.

'What do you want, Elf?' he asks.

Lex continues, 'Please, listen to me. I understand the pull to try to save the person you love most in the world. Believe me, I do. Mallena, she promised you the choker, didn't she? Please understand that the choker isn't going to stop your wife from dying.'

Hoffman looks up at Lex. 'The choker isn't for her . . . It's for me.'

Lex gasps. 'What? That's what it's for? You're running? You're doing all this just to run away from the pain of your wife dying? You . . . *coward*!'

'GET THEM OUT!' Hoffman shouts and then turns around, walking fast ahead.

Your heart feels heavy and your stomach feels as if it is full of tears. You watch as two SAMs carry Blake's lifeless body and another carries Anka over his shoulder. The Minotaurs carry your friends as if they are objects, like a filthy mop or a bag of rubbish. Your eyes well up as you see them being carried past you, wishing you could shout out, wishing you could at least ask them to be more respectful. But you know that doing so would only put you and your friends in even more danger, so you keep your mouth shut.

The SAMs escort you down a long, winding staircase, lit by flaming torches. Your head is spinning, and your vision is blurry from exhaustion, hunger and grief. At the bottom of the staircase is a long hallway, also lit by flickering torches. You pass numerous paintings of various magical creatures – elves, witches, sorcerers, dragons – and realise that all of them look as if they've been photographed with a black-and-white filter. You look around you and realise that everyone, including the SAMs and your friends, look grey, as if having arrived from an old film. An old clock you pass in the hallway shows the time: 11.15 p.m. You have forty-five minutes to prevent the end of the world and the situation could not be less favourable.

You lower your head in shame and keep walking until you approach a large wooden door, shaped like a giant book. Hoffman walks to the door and knocks.

To your surprise, the book-shaped door says in a hushed whisper, 'Welcome to the library. Please keep your conversations quiet.' The door then opens with a barely audible creak.

Hoffman is the first to step inside, followed by the rest of the SAMs. When you are escorted inside, you squint against the bright chandelier lights. Mallena stands at the far end of the enormous room, which, you notice, is shaped like a giant star. Her dress no longer looks scarlet, but rather a dark shade of grey. Her choker blinks a light grey colour. She is smiling, holding a handful of chokers in her hands.

'Hoffman,' she says. 'Come forward.'

Hoffman approaches her and bows.

Mallena continues, 'You have served me well. You have been a faithful servant all these years. Your loyalty deserves a reward.' She hands one of the chokers to him. 'May this bring you the relief you seek from your suffering.'

Hoffman takes the choker and bows. 'Thank you, ma'am.'

'Coward!' Michael yells, trying to free himself from the four SAMs who are struggling to hold him back.

Hoffman turns to look at him and you see the big Minotaur's face. His eyes show you the depth of his heartbroken soul. You can feel his grief in your own heart and you can feel his shame in your stomach. Hoffman swallows but says nothing.

Mallena approaches you and thrusts a choker into your hands. 'I believe this one is yours. You left it at the prison.'

'I'm not putting it on and you can't make me,' you say.

'We'll see,' she says with a smile, before walking up to Talia. 'You, my dear, are the first and only one ever to break a choker. Tell me – how did you get it off?'

'I guess your magic isn't as strong as you thought, Mallena,' Talia says. 'You rule by the black magic of intimidation and fear, but these don't stand a chance against the white magic of compassion and courage.'

'Ah, I should have guessed,' Mallena says, turning to Eribelle. 'You still think the Moon Tradition can cure everyone.'

'It can,' Eribelle says firmly. 'If everyone was compassionate and kind, then none of this would have happened and our friends would still be alive.'

'I used to think so too,' Mallena says. 'I am truly sorry about your friends. I never wanted anyone to get hurt. And if everyone was wearing a choker, there would be no emotion, there would be no hatred. Opening your heart to the world only adds to pain and suffering.'

'And your answer is to numb everyone's emotions?' Eribelle snaps.

'Yes! I am saving them, whereas your method is adding to their suffering.'

'Your chokers are killing them!' Celeste shouts.

Mallena turns to look at her, frowning. 'I don't expect a witch to understand sorcery, but know this, witch: these chokers are for your own good.' She thrusts a choker into Celeste's hands, then Eribelle's, and then the rest of the legion members'.

'May I ask you a question, my lady?' Abbott asks her.

'You just did, Abbott, but you may ask me another.'

'Thank you, my lady. Please tell me, why do you care for the ogre? You gave him a choker along with the others. Ogres are all scum and don't deserve—'

'Silence!' Mallena snaps. 'I will not have such talk in Here. You are suspended for one week with no pay.'

'But—'

'Out!'

Abbott storms out, murmuring something about imps having the right idea, and slams the door behind him. The door makes a shushing sound in response.

Mallena turns to face all of you. 'Now, I suggest you all put on your chokers.'

Michael throws his choker on the ground and spits on it. No one else moves.

'I see,' Mallena says. 'OK. Have it your way.' She then turns to face the SAMs. 'Any of you without a choker will need to leave for your own safety.'

The SAMs bow and exit one by one, ignoring the irritable murmuring of the library door. A few moments later, only Mallena, Hoffman, you and the legion remain in the library.

'Last chance,' Mallena says to you. 'Put on the choker.'

'No,' you say.

'Anka knew this would happen. She told me that today would be the day that you would be forever changed. It looks like she was right.'

You feel as if your head has been dunked in a bucket of ice. *What? She knew? She knew that I would lose?* Anger, betrayal and deep hurt penetrate every ounce of your being.

'Well?' Mallena asks.

'No,' you say.

'Have it your way. But know that at any time you want to make it stop, all you have to do is put on the choker. That goes for all of you,' she says, addressing the legion. 'It doesn't hurt, and if you put it on, you will never suffer again.'

None of you move. Mallena concentrates and conjures up a dark maelstrom of revolving clouds with her hands.

You start to hear familiar voices. *'You are a fraud! You are a failure. You are going to let everyone down!'*

'The Fusion clouds!' you shout.

The dragopurrs, evidently made uncomfortable by the heavy cloud, lower themselves to the ground and whimper.

'Quickly! We need to start the Moon Tradition!' Eribelle shouts.

All of you run toward her and form a circle facing one another.

'We need to make sure we have enough power to fight this,' she says.

The only way to attempt to cast the white magic of the Moon Tradition against such a large cloud of Fusion darkness is to make sure that you have a total of at least 50 points combined across the categories of Wisdom, Inner Strength and Courage. In addition, you also need to have at least 10 points in each category.

If you meet both of these conditions – a total of 50 points or more with a minimum of 10 points in each of the categories – proceed to page 169.

If you do not have enough points to face the Fusion spell and are too devastated to continue, you will need to go back to page 32 to try again, by making different decisions to build your wisdom, inner strength and courage to be able to face Mallena and withstand her dark magic.

Moon Tradition

Gain 5 inner strength and 5 wisdom points

We are all born with a natural desire to be loved and accepted by others. When that doesn't happen, we might look for ways to be accepted, to fit in, to belong. Sometimes our very fear of being rejected or disliked can become the root of our emotional struggles. We might get extremely depressed, have overwhelming anxiety attacks, or fixate on certain thoughts or behaviours as a way of struggling with the idea that we might somehow be 'unlovable' or 'not good enough', 'not worthy of love and acceptance'. This is why we might fixate on being 'perfect', on being 'thin enough', 'attractive enough' or 'accomplished enough'.

Sometimes we might even alienate others because we are too afraid of them finding out how 'damaged', 'messed up' or 'imperfect' we really are, believing that if they truly knew us, they would reject us. Unfortunately, doing this can create the very outcome we are trying to avoid. More specifically, when we avoid others for the fear of rejection, we are more likely to end up being alone.

Furthermore, we might sometimes engage in certain behaviours or rituals as a way to cover up our fear of being rejected or unloved. For example, if there is something about ourselves that we are ashamed of, such as our appearance or skills, we might try to cover up these perceived imperfections with humour, sarcasm, perfectionism, anger or chronic worry as a way to problem-solve or avoid these uncomfortable thoughts and feelings.

What often arises when we fuse with thoughts, such as 'I'm not good enough' or 'I am unlovable', is shame. In fact, we are more likely to harshly shame and criticise ourselves, and the more

25

anxious, depressed or angry we might feel. The worse we feel, the less distress we can tolerate, sometimes becoming irritable or struggling to cope with situations, which under other circumstances would not bother us as much.

Unchecked and ignored, shame emotions can potentially become disruptive, creating thoughts such as: 'I'm a failure', 'I'm worthless' and 'I'm not good enough'. The antidote for shame is called *self-compassion,* which is the essence of the Moon Tradition.

Self-compassion refers to finding a way to love, accept and support yourself in the same kind and caring way as you would care for a dear friend or a favourite family member. Some people believe that self-compassion is a weakness or a way to pity ourselves. In reality, self-compassion requires great strength and courage to face our difficult emotions, instead of running away from them. It allows us to care for ourselves, and promote healing and connection with others, which is different from pity (an emotion that increases alienation and disconnection, as well as reduces healing).

Others believe that self-compassion will not allow them to be as motivated as using harsh words and stringent discipline. In fact, self-shaming (for example, one that I've often used on myself is: 'Get to the gym, you fat pig') can initially increase motivation because it creates shame and fear. However, when we have a setback (for example, if we indulged in an unhealthy food or skipped the gym), the harsh self-critical voice is more likely to elevate shame so much that we are more likely to give up than to continue trying. On the other hand, self-compassion uses kind reminders of what is important to you (for example, health) in order to continue motivating you over and over again, even if you've had a setback. It encourages you to follow your goals and life-directions without putting you down.

Proceed to page 91 to continue learning about the self-compassion practice – the Moon Tradition.

Werewolf Identity

Lose 10 wisdom points

You are now an angry, raging werewolf. You forget what you stand for. You forget yourself and start acting purely based on your new condition. This means that when you become angry as a result of the increased adrenaline surge during your transformation, you are likely to become aggressive and violent. You act based on your emotion as opposed to what matters most to you.

Proceed to page 100.

Anka and Blake are laid to rest in the woods next to Java. As their bodies are lowered into the ground, Lex and Hoffman play 'Midnight Rain'. You notice your heart feeling heavy with grief, but also light with love and compassion for everyone around you. It reminds you of eating bittersweet chocolate.

Michael is the first to pick up a shovel. He takes a breath and then throws a shovelful of earth down on to the caskets. You go next, your heart crying inside. You lift up a patch of earth with the shovel and gently allow the dirt to cascade down, blanketing your deceased friends with your love.

When both Blake and Anka are buried, you all stand in a circle. No one speaks for a while. No one needs to. You are all feeling the same emotions, and in your grief and in your hearts you are all connected. You feel a strangely comforting feeling from this connection.

Out of the corner of your eye you notice movement. You turn in its direction and see a tiny hedgehog with a missing back paw. He has an apple slice attached to his spines.

'It's Yozhik!' you realise. 'Anka's hedgehog!'

Yozhik climbs up on top on Anka's grave, rolls to remove the apple slice and places it down on the fresh ground. He then cuddles the apple slice with his three paws and lies down to sleep. Your eyes water at this sight. Next to you, Michael and Katrina both sniffle as they are holding hands, the dragopurrs nuzzling against their arms.

Celeste is the first to break the silence. 'I would like to take this moment to honour Anka, for always being our voice of reason. As well as Blake, without whom we would not have figured out a way to break the chokers and stop Mallena. And lastly . . .' She sighs. 'I would like to honour Java, the funniest bird I've ever known.' She smiles through her tears. 'I know you'll keep them smiling wherever your wings take you.'

'Here, Here,' you all say.

Celeste blows her nose, sniffles again, and takes a large swig from her coffee mug.

'And I would like to congratulate Eribelle,' Lex says. 'I could not think of a better individual to take Mallena's place.'

Eribelle blushes. 'Thank you, Lex. I am honoured to have you and Michael join our tactical forces at the consulate.'

Michael smiles. 'I guess there are great things ahead for all of us.'

'Please, uh, will you, uh, come to my restaurant when, uh, it opens?' Gherk asks.

'You bet, Gherk,' Katrina says, and gives him a big hug.

'Well . . . I'd better get going,' Hoffman says. 'I promised Carmen I would take her to her appointment.'

'Take care, man,' Michael says. 'Let us know if you need anything.'

'Thanks,' Hoffman says, shaking Michael's hand. He then turns to you. 'Thank you. For everything.'

'For what?' you ask in surprise.

'You've given me my life back. It's interesting how a person can really change the course of another's life and might never know it. I wanted you to know.'

'Thank you,' you say, feeling your cheeks blush.

'What should I do?' he asks you.

'What do you mean?'

'When I get home, how do I help her? What should I say? How can I take her pain away?'

You step toward him and place your hand on the Minotaur's heart. 'You can't, Hoffman. You can't take away her pain. Take the pressure off yourself to fix it or to take this away from her. Just be with her.'

His eyes are full of tears but he breathes along with you, his breaths slowing down now. 'Just be with her?' he asks, his voice breaking.

'Just be with her,' you repeat. 'That is your only job.'

His eyes widen. 'And what if she doesn't make it?'

'No matter what, she will always be right Here,' you say, pointing to his heart.

He sniffles again and then nods. 'OK . . . OK. I can do this. For her. For Carmen.' He envelops you in a giant hug. 'Thanks.'

You all watch him leave.

'What will happen to Mallena?' you ask Eribelle.

'Her magic has been frozen. She will not be able to use it until she is deemed ready to do so. I sent her to study mindfulness with Serena again. Only now she will also be learning and practising self-compassion. I am hoping that this will help her reduce her empathic distress and heartbreak, and will hopefully help rehabilitate her.'

'And what about me?' you ask. 'What will happen to me?'

Eribelle takes your hand. 'My dear friend. There is so much more work to be done. This adventure is only the beginning. Now that you understand your core values and the things that keep you back from honouring them, there are infinite opportunities for you to be involved in making the world a better place. Every day is another chance to respond to your own call to an adventure. Every time you feel scared, depressed or insecure, you have choices to make – to avoid the situation or to follow your core values, to practise mindfulness and self-compassion, and to remember who you are and what you stand for. Always look for an opportunity to help others and to support yourself in your own heroic journey. Remember, you are the Chosen One for a reason. Remember that what you do matters. Remember that you can make a big difference in the lives of others.

'If you ever feel stuck or overwhelmed, you can always ask for help, you can always ask yourself what you stand for. Remember to find your feet and to connect with your heart. Practise the white magic of the Moon Tradition. And above all, know that anytime you need, you can always be right Here.'

'So, what's next?' you ask.

'I think you already know,' Celeste says.

You nod, take a breath and close your eyes.

When you open them again you are back home, back in your room. The usual smells and sounds of your surroundings are strangely comforting. You feel your feet as they touch the floor.

I am Here, you remind yourself with a smile.

<u>YOUR QUEST ENDS HERE, BUT DO RETURN TO THE START AND SEE IF THERE ARE OTHER CHOICES YOU COULD MAKE</u>.

There are loud growls outside, like lionesses attacking their prey.

'What is that?' you ask, finally able to breathe.

'Oh, it's my dragopurrs,' Katrina answers. 'Poor things, they are probably bored.'

'What are dragopurrs?'

'They are basically dragon-sized cats,' Katrina explains. 'They fly and they can spit fire like their reptilian relatives, but other than that, dragopurrs are mostly feline. Would you like to meet them?'

'Um . . . sure.' You are not sure.

'Just don't pet their stomachs and you should be OK.'

You follow Katrina outside. *Is meeting giant fire-spitting cats a great idea right now?*

The growling gets louder as you step outside. Two black and white cats, big enough to swallow several tigers, are wrestling each other. Their massive wings are covered in scales.

'These are the Tuxedo twins,' Katrina says proudly. 'The slightly smaller one with the white cheek is Hera, and the other one is Hektor. They're only six months, so they're still babies.'

'Only six months?' you ask in amazement.

Hera manages to break herself free when Hektor swats at his sister's face. She leans back, dodging, then lowers her bottom and her ears, shaking side to side before pouncing on her brother. The two hiss and growl playfully, sometimes spitting fire and occasionally nibbling at each other's ears.

Katrina looks at them with the adoration of a mother watching her children play. 'They're a little frisky right now, but perhaps when they've calmed down a bit you might be able to pet them.'

'They are yours?'

'Yes and no. I am a veterinarian and people often bring me injured animals they find, or ones that need looking after.' She points to the dragopurrs who are currently stalking a pack of vultures directly above them. 'These two were found by the locals when they were just a week old. Their mother must have abandoned them and I took them in. They were barely bigger than I was back then. Now look at them! They seem to grow by the minute.'

Just then Hera leaps up into the air, catching the smaller of the vultures' wings in her mouth. The bird attempts to flee but the feline's teeth pull it to the ground. Once Hera lands with her prey in her mouth, Hektor jumps on the vulture, trying to claim it as his own. There are growls, hisses and protests from all parties as Katrina grabs a garden hose.

'Bad kitties!' Katrina says as she sprays the dragopurrs. Both felines jump in alarm, giving the vulture a brief moment of freedom. The next moment the bird is up in the air again, flying toward his flock.

You find yourself smiling.

Katrina turns to you. 'I know that this is very hard for you. I can't even imagine the pressure you're under to lead this mission.'

You consider her words before responding. 'Thank you. The truth is that I have no idea what I'm doing. I can't help but think that there's been a huge mistake and I feel like the biggest fraud in the world, you know?'

'Ah.' She smiles. 'The good ol' fraud syndrome.'

You stare at her. 'You know about that?'

'When I first arrived Here and the word got out that I'm a veterinarian, people started bringing me creatures I'd never seen before and knew nothing about. The dragopurrs in particular are still a challenge because they fly and need to be trained, and well . . .' She blushes. 'I'm terribly afraid of heights. So . . . yeah. Feeling like the biggest fraud in the world on a daily basis.'

'It's just that Michael . . .'

'Don't listen to Michael,' she says. 'He can be a bit rough sometimes. I honestly think it's because of what he went through during the war.'

'What happened to him?' you ask.

'He lost his entire squad in one day. Based on what I know, he sent them to scout out the area and they were all ambushed. Didn't even stand a chance. Torn to shreds. He barely managed to get away but he was the only one. He still blames himself.'

'That's horrible,' you say, your heart heavy, feeling for Michael.

'So don't take what he says to heart.'

'It's hard not to,' you say. 'I feel like he's testing me.'

'I know it feels that way. He is just making sure your intentions are good. Look, we are all in this together. I know it's hard for you. But you're not alone. We are all on this mission with you.'

You take a deep breath. 'Thank you. I really appreciate it.'

And with that, the two of you walk back inside.

The living room is mostly dark now, except for the dim glow from Michael's laptop. You manage to make out Anka's and Lex's shapes as they are kneeling over Celeste. The witch is lying on the couch with a towel over her face. Her raven, Java, sits by her head, gently petting her with his wing.

'What's wrong?' you ask them.

'Shh,' Lex says, getting up and then pulling you to another side of the room. 'Celeste gets these terrible migraines when she over-exerts herself, like she did with the freeze spell. She will need some time to recover.'

Celeste moans on the other side of the room. 'Please . . . please . . . stop . . . talking. And please . . . stop . . . typing.' Her speech seems laboured and, judging by her voice, she seems to be in a lot of pain.

'Sorry,' Lex whispers in a barely audible whisper as Michael, seemingly frustrated, closes the laptop with a loud snap.

'Aah!' Celeste screams, covering her head with her arms.

Michael grunts and storms out of the room. The room is entirely dark now and Lex gently guides you out into the kitchen. There, Gherk is working on breakfast. Bacon sizzles as he mixes several dozen eggs in an enormous pot. You sit at the table next to Lex.

'Everything smells delicious, Gherk,' Lex says to the ogre. 'Do you need any help?'

'Oh, uh, that's, uh, very kind . . . I, uh . . .' He looks at the bacon, his eyes widening in alarm. 'No, no, no, no!' he shouts, grabbing the bacon-filled frying pan by the handle and throwing both the bacon and the pan in the bin. He then turns to the sink and begins washing his hands quickly and urgently, scrubbing them so hard that you notice some of the blisters, developed no doubt from the frequent washing, begin to bleed. He is panting, counting his washes in exasperation.

'Is he OK?' you ask Lex. 'I mean . . . I guess that's a dumb question. He's clearly not OK, at least not right now.'

'He used to own a restaurant in Venice. One of his patrons died from a peanut allergy after eating something cooked on a frying pan that wasn't carefully washed after it was used to make stir-fry peanut sauce. Broke poor Gherk's heart. He wasn't even working that day but he blames himself for it. Ever since it happened, he's become extremely cautious about washing all his cooking supplies and his hands over and over. And if he doesn't think that something is clean enough or if he believes that the food he is making somehow got contaminated, he throws it all out.'

'Oh, wow,' you say, feeling the crushing sensation in your own heart and knotting in your stomach, as if feeling Gherk's guilt.

'It gets worse,' Lex continues. 'He was throwing out so much food that he lost his restaurant, his wife later left him, and none of his old friends will speak to him because they think he's "mental". We are all he's got now.'

You look away from Lex so as not to show your eyes tearing up. You find yourself feeling both sad for Gherk and also embarrassed that his story has affected you so much.

'You seem like a good caretaker for your friends,' you tell Lex. 'The legion is lucky to have a girl like you.'

'Thank you,' Lex says. 'Though technically I am not a girl.'

'Oh, sorry. Elf, I mean.'

'No. I mean, that's true, but what I meant is that elves have no gender.'

'Oh! I'm sorry for assuming.'

Over by the kitchen sink Gherk is still washing his hands as he frantically counts: '. . . eighty-six, eighty-seven, eighty-nine . . .' He stops. 'Damn it!' He pours a bunch of soap on his hands, sniffling, wiping his eyes with his sleeve, and begins to wash again. 'One, two, three . . .'

It takes Gherk over twenty-five minutes to finish scrubbing his hands. Finally, he takes out an enormous new pan from his apron and, after thoroughly washing it as well, places it on the stove. You find yourself wondering if Gherk's apron is enchanted to be bigger on the inside in order to fit all his kitchen supplies.

Celeste walks into the kitchen, Java sitting on her shoulder. You notice that Celeste's eyes are red and she has bags under them. She looks awfully pale and stern.

'How are you feeling?' you ask her, jumping to your feet.

'Getting better, thanks,' she says weakly as she takes a large gulp from her mug. She turns to Gherk. 'Thank you so much for making us breakfast. Just a friendly reminder – Lex and I are vegetarian, and Talia has her blood vials, so she should be all set.' She turns back to you. 'Do you have any dietary restrictions?'

After breakfast, everyone seems to be in a much better mood, including you. Anka helps Gherk with the dishes and then sits down next to you. She is holding a small hedgehog. He appears to be missing one of his back paws.

'Yours?' you ask her.

'Yes.' She smiles. 'His name is Yozhik. Do you vant to pet him?'

'Sure,' you say and gently pet the hedgehog until it crawls onto your lap and falls asleep.

'I sink he likes you,' Anka says, smiling at you again.

'So, what do we do, captain?' Michael asks you with a smirk on his face.

'I'm not a captain.' You blush with embarrassment, handing Yozhik back to Anka.

'Well, you're supposed to be leading this mission. So, in my book, that makes you captain.'

You feel a familiar surge of self-doubt, but Katrina's encouraging smile helps you feel a little more confident.

'OK,' you say. 'What do we know about Mallena so far?'

'She is an evil sorceress, she is in charge of the Magic Consulate, she's in charge of Here, and recently people have been disappearing,' Anka says flatly.

'She is evil and always was,' Celeste adds.

'That's not exactly accurate,' Talia corrects her. 'Mallena actually used to be quite lovely. I even interned with her for a while. When she was elected as the director of the consulate, it really seemed that she truly had everyone's best interests at heart.'

'So what changed?' you ask.

'No one knows. One day she just—' Talia begins but Michael interrupts her.

'She just went all kinds of awful overnight.'

'Stop interrupting me!' Talia shouts at him, banging her fist on the table.

'Stop being so freaking sensitive!' Michael yells back.

Talia rolls her eyes and huffs. She glares at Michael, who rolls his eyes back at her. Talia continues: 'As I was saying, one day she just . . . changed. She suddenly became obsessed with controlling everyone's emotions rather than encouraging us to experience them like she used to. I heard that she even offers a way to turn off all negative emotions to those who serve her.'

'Can she really do that?' you ask. The idea of being forever free from overwhelming anxiety, insecurity, depression and shame sounds rather appealing.

'I don't know for sure. All any of us know is that since she started this campaign to make everyone into her little emotional slaves, people have started disappearing from Here or becoming somehow inhuman. And if Anka's prophecy is accurate, then in one week, unless we stop her, this world dies.'

'Does that mean we will die too?' you ask, dreading the answer.

Everyone turns to Anka.

She shrugs. 'I do not know. It is possible zat a part of us vill die. But I do not know for sure and I do not vant to find out.'

'Do we know what caused that change in Mallena?' you ask.

'No idea,' says Talia. Everyone else shakes their head.

'Is there anything that might have occurred around the time that change happened?' you ask.

'Don't know that either,' Talia says.

'I may know someone who might,' says Michael. 'Serena, the Mermaid of the Black Lake. She and Mallena used to meditate together every week. I used to be a part of Intel for the security team who had to escort Mallena to the Black Lake. On several occasions, I had to help escort her there myself. And then one day Mallena just stopped going. It might have been a coincidence but . . . it happened around the time that she started changing. I didn't really put the pieces together . . . You know, it might be worthwhile to talk to Serena.'

'How do we find her?' you ask.

Michael shivers. 'The Black Lake is in the Dark Forest. It is full of dark magic. When I used to escort Mallena there, she used her powers to shield all of us from the hags, ghouls and other beasts. Without that kind of protection, we don't really stand a chance.'

The others in the room exchange glances.

'Is there any other way of getting there?' you ask Anka. 'Can we somehow transport there the same way as when you brought me Here?'

She shakes her head. 'Sadly, no. It does not vork like zat. I can only bring people into zis vorld but not to different parts of it.'

'What about you, Celeste?' you ask. 'Are there spells that you can use that might help us get past the creatures of the Dark Forest?'

'I can try,' Celeste says. 'I will do what's necessary.'

'Absolutely not!' Anka says firmly. 'You are already veak as it is.'

'I'll be OK,' Celeste argues.

Anka does not seem to be convinced and neither are you.

'OK.' You turn to Katrina. 'How about the dragopurrs? Can they fly us out there?'

Katrina shakes her head. 'Unfortunately not. They still have a lot of training to do.'

Michael rolls his eyes at her. 'They would have been trained by now if someone would have just got over herself and done her bloody job!' He shoots a nasty look at Katrina, who storms out of the room.

'Katrina!' Celeste runs after her.

'Why are you always so mean?' Talia asks him, frowning.

'Because this is war!' he shouts. 'We are wasting time talking about *feelings* and being all *sensitive* when this world is apparently scheduled to end in a week! So yes, Talia, I'm going to be mean; I'm going to be whatever I have to be to prevent that from happening!'

He gets up from his chair and stands in the corner, feeling the wall with his hands. The room seems to be drowning in his fury.

A few moments later Celeste and Katrina return to the room. Katrina's eyes are red and her head is bowed low. She takes a breath before she speaks. 'I will start training them to transport people.'

Michael turns around to face her. 'You do realise this means that you'd have to—'

'I know what this means,' she says firmly, looking up at him. 'It will take some time but I will work with them as much as I can.'

'So, then, what are our options?' Celeste asks you, and every-one stares at you again, waiting for your response, waiting for your lead.

Once more the words 'you are a fraud' show up in your mind. You take notice of them, along with the feelings of anxiety and insecurity you are experiencing. You allow these thoughts and emotions to be present while focusing on your mission. For what feels like the first time in your life, you are not held back by your insecurities. You are ready to meet your challenge.

'We can't wait until Katrina finishes training the dragopurrs,' you say. 'It sounds like our only option might be to face whatever lives in the Dark Forest. We'll just have to trust ourselves and each other to meet whatever challenge we face.'

'Preach!' shouts Java as the others laugh.

'I can lead the way, though I wish I still had my maps,' Michael says. 'I knew I should have brought those when I emptied out my office at the consulate.'

'I might have something that can help,' Celeste says, turning to her raven. 'Java, can you please get me my Presence Maps? I think they are in the bedroom.'

The raven spreads his wings and flies off to another room as Celeste takes another gulp of her coffee.

'Do you ever think that you might be drinking too much of that?' Lex asks her.

Celeste shrugs. 'It helps me function and get things done.'

'Excuse me, uh, Celeste,' Gherk says. 'You, uh, mentioned that, uh, these are, uh, Presence Maps? What, uh, are the, uh, Presence Maps?'

'A Presence Map shows you where you are on the map in real time, so that you can see where you need to go.'

Java flies back into the living room with a roll of parchment in his claw. Celeste takes another swig of her coffee, then takes the parchment from Java and unrolls it on the table.

The map shows a dark green forest in the north, a tall volcanic mountain in the south, a gothic-looking castle in the east, and Lex and Celeste's house in the west, the focal point of the map. Above the house is a balloon, almost like an inverted teardrop, that reads: *You are HERE.*

41

'As we move, the presence indicator –' she points to the balloon on the map – 'will move too, showing us where we are at all times. Knowing where we are will make it easier to figure out where we need to go.'

'That's, uh, clever,' says Gherk.

'Better pack for at least a few days' worth,' Celeste suggests. 'We don't know how long it will be before we get back.'

'*If* we get back,' Michael mutters with a frown.

It takes everyone nearly an hour to get ready. Celeste packs a bunch of coffee creamers, as well as coffee cakes, coffee-covered almonds, and a book called *A Thousand and One Ways to Make the Perfect Cup of Coffee.* Michael packs up his emergency kit, a sword and several knives. Talia stocks up her portable cooler with several vials of fresh blood, while Lex fills the quiver with arrows and packs a cloak. You all would have left sooner if Gherk didn't need to rewash his pots and hands before leaving.

While the other members of the Legion of Coeur are packing and getting ready to leave, Katrina begins training the dragopurrs. Using a clicker and large pieces of salmon, she teaches the felines to associate the sounds of the clicker with receiving the salmon treat. The dragopurrs are quick to learn this and in no time orient their heads toward the clicker and run toward her, ready to receive their treat. They eat it purring, tilting their head from side to side, and occasionally growling at one another as a precaution to stay away from their food.

'Here,' Michael says, handing Katrina an enormous white teddy bear. 'For the cats, you know?'

'Ah, thank you!' Katrina grabs the teddy bear and hugs Michael. He looks wildly uncomfortable and stiff but does not push her away.

'I will call him Snowball,' Katrina says when she lets go of Michael. She then turns to the dragopurrs. 'Look! A toy. Do you want it?'

Hektor bats the bear with his paw as Hera pounces on him and

43

wrestles Snowball away from him. She then picks up the fluffy toy with her teeth, so that it looks like she is carrying a kitten, and growls at Hektor as he tries to approach.

'I think they like it.' Katrina smiles.

When everyone is packed and ready to go, you and the legion head out of the headquarters and into the forest. Celeste and Michael are leading at the front, using the Presence Map as a guide. You peek over Celeste's shoulder and notice that indeed, as the legion moves, the presence indicator moves with it, indicating your current location in real time.

Less than twenty minutes into the journey, Hektor and Hera stop following the legion and lie down for a nap. They stretch out in a sunny spot near a large oak tree and cuddle up.

'No, no, no,' Katrina says. 'We are not stopping for a nap. Up! Let's go.'

But the dragopurrs ignore her and begin to wash each other, purring loudly.

'Oh, great!' Michael says sarcastically. 'I see we are going to go far now.'

'Leave them alone,' Katrina snaps back. 'They've been training for over an hour.'

'Maybe they wouldn't have needed so much training if you trained them a long time ago like I asked you to. And maybe they wouldn't have been so tired if you hadn't overfed them!'

'Enough!' Anka shouts. 'Ve have no time to argue. Ve have two choices: eizer ve all vait for ze dragopurrs to be ready or ve leave Katrina here viz zem.'

Michael, Katrina, Celeste and Talia begin arguing as you once again feel useless and insecure. You sigh and lower your head, putting your hands in your pockets. You feel your keys in your right pocket and play with them.

Suddenly, you get an idea. You take out your keys from your pocket, grabbing the keychain – a small laser pointer. You point it at the base of the tree, near the dragopurrs, and click it on, then shake the pointer gently to stimulate motion.

The dragopurrs pay it no attention at first, but then Hera happens to look in the direction of the tree. Her ears perk up when she notices the little moving red dot. The next moment, she jumps up on to her paws, not taking her eyes off the moving target. Her tail moves from side to side, and she pounces on to the light. You let go of the button and the laser dot vanishes as Hera lifts up her paws in the hopes of examining her target. Not seeing one, she looks back to Hektor in distress, meowing. Hektor, who appears to have missed the laser pointer action, looks confused and sleepy.

You shine the light again, this time between the two felines. Hektor's eyes narrow, zooming in on the dot like camera lenses. Both felines pounce toward the light, bumping into each other. This doesn't seem to deter them from the game, however, and they look up to you, seeing you holding the pointer. Hera meows at you, as if requesting that you continue the game.

Clever kittens!

'Katrina, look!' You show her the dragopurrs' reaction.

'Not bad, captain.' Michael grins.

The legion is back on track, with Katrina leading the felines with your laser pointer.

It is late afternoon when the presence indicator shifts close to the Black Lake. The trees are becoming thicker and you notice the strange shapes they begin to take. Some look like creepy skeletons, whispering at you from the shadows. Others seem as if they are ready to grab you with their spiky branches. Some trees creak as they rock back and forth, despite the apparent lack of wind. Shadows appear to be spreading from the trees out toward you.

'Why is it getting so dark?' you ask.

'Because we are getting close to dark magic,' Michael replies. He then addresses everyone. 'All right. We need to keep our eyes open. Don't believe what you see and what you hear. There are enchantments here to scare you and to keep you back from your mission.'

'What kinds of enchantments?' Talia asks.

'There are spells to make you second-guess yourself. There are also creatures to intimidate you, to stop you. There are—'

45

'Michael!' Lex shouts.

You turn. Lex is pointing to a tall, thin, faceless woman standing between the trees. Her clothes and skin tone make it seem as if she is a part of the tree, her white hair billowing in the wind. The woman hisses at all of you.

Talia, Gherk and Katrina gasp as the dragopurrs arch their backs and hiss back.

'Wha-what is that?' you ask.

'Some kind of a hag,' Celeste responds.

'What does it want?' you ask, not taking your eyes off the creepy woman between the trees.

'I have no idea,' Celeste says, shuddering.

'Gah!' you scream when another hag suddenly appears in front of you. 'Michael! What do I do?'

'I . . . I don't know. I've never seen them before . . .'

'Ah!' you scream as the hag grabs your right arm.

Faceless though it may be, you feel as if it is somehow staring at you. And then it speaks: 'Fraud! You are a fraud. Once everyone finds out how little you actually know, they will abandon you. They will hate you.'

'Die, you evil . . .' Michael tries to stab the hag with his sword but she pays him no notice. He tries again and again but the hag won't release your arm. 'Let go!' he yells and tries to stab the woman again, until another hag grabs both his arms and speaks without a mouth.

'You should have protected them. Those people died because of you. You let them down.'

Michael looks at the hag. For a moment he tries to move but he seems to have lost his willpower. You recognise the look on his face – his glassy eyes, his droopy face.

It's guilt. And shame.

The hags don't give up. 'They had families,' Michael's hag shouts at him. 'What do you have to say to their children?'

Katrina tries to pull him out of it. 'Michael, don't listen to them.' However, she is now facing yet another Faceless.

'You are going to let everyone down. You are a coward! You are an embarrassment! This mission is going to fail because you are too chicken to face your fears.'

Soon enough everyone is facing hags of their own. The Faceless seem to be excellent at scaring all of you with what you are most afraid will happen in the future or at shaming you about your past.

One nasty Faceless grabs Lex, whispering loud enough for you to hear: 'Your father was so embarrassed by you when you froze up playing the guitar. Your mother never accepted your sexuality. It would have been better if you had just killed yourself that night but you couldn't even do that right. You brought so much shame to the family. Just do the honourable thing and kill yourself already.'

Another one is torturing Talia: 'Your grandmother was right – you are fat! And disgusting!'

You feel that the others want to give up. You feel it too. Even the dragopurrs have buried their heads in each other's fur.

Then the creatures begin to drag you deeper into the darkness. 'Come with me.'

'We need to get out of here!' you yell.

'HERE!' Anka shouts, grasping her chest with both of her hands. 'Look at your arms!'

You struggle to understand but do what she says. When you glance down at your arms, you see the little balloon. *You are Here.*

And you understand.

'Look at your MESS marks!' you yell to the others. 'The hags are trying to scare us with the future or hold us back with our past. But we are in the present.'

'Do not let zem take you avay!' Anka orders. 'Keep looking at your marks.'

'Come with me!' the hags yell at those they have grabbed. 'Come with me or you will die.'

If you decide to go with the hags, turn to page 168.

If you decide to focus on your MESS marks to stay in the present moment, turn to page 69.

'Come with me!' the hag yells at you.

'No,' you say. 'I'm staying right Here.'

'You will die! You will be destroyed! You will . . .' The hag tries to carry you away again.

'Right now, at this moment, I am Here. My feet are on the ground. The world is not yet ending. And I am staying right Here,' you persist.

The hag roars at you and tries to pull you, but you notice that its grip is not nearly as tight as it was just a few moments ago. The firmer and more grounded you feel in the present moment, the weaker the hag's hold of you seems to be. Until finally it disappears, and so do its sisters.

Once everything settles, and the tight pressure releases from your chest and stomach, the others begin to unwind, as if finally freed from a binding spell. The dragopurrs are slow to rise, their paws shaking, their movements uncertain, their young age now quite apparent despite their enormous bodies. Katrina kneels next to them and pets them. The felines' pupils are still large from fear but they slowly settle down.

'Is everyone all right?' Celeste asks.

Some groans and nods confirm that everyone is unharmed.

Celeste then comforts the distressed Java. 'Don't you listen to them. I would never trade you in for a cat. You are the perfect familiar, the best one I've ever had.'

You kneel next to Katrina. 'May I pet them?'

'Sure,' she says. 'Here, have them smell your hand first, so they can see that they can trust you.'

49

You extend your hand to them; Hektor sniffs it and then Hera does. They lower their heads, as if inviting you to pet them. You take turns petting them, feeling their soft fur on your hands. A few minutes later, the felines purr loudly, head-butting your hands to demand more attention.

When everyone seems to feel better, Celeste unrolls the map and leads the group forward. As you walk next to her, you notice once again that the presence indicator moves as your group moves, reminding anyone who looks at it that 'You are HERE'. There is something oddly comforting about it. It is as if it reminds you that at this very moment, you are not attacked by the Strah, the hags or your deepest, darkest fears. You are Here, in the forest, with the rest of the legion, heading toward the large black circle on the map that is titled the Black Lake.

Turn to page 128.

Experiential Avoidance Curse

Lose 3 courage points

You're stuck attacking monsters as you avoid a personal confrontation. They will always come back and you will just have to fight more of them.

Attempts we make to avoid or control our emotional experiences are called *experiential avoidance*. Just as with the monsters you chose to run from, here, experiential avoidance can provide short-term relief. For example, bingeing on ice cream, your favourite TV show or substance (such as alcohol) instead of working on a school or work project might temporarily make us feel better. However, in the long-term, experiential avoidance will usually make us feel worse. Our monsters will multiply.

Think about it: did your past attempts to control how you feel actually make you feel better or worse in the long-term? Most people report the latter. For example, if someone (let's say a girl named Sally Unicorn) is struggling with social anxiety, she might refuse to attend a friend's birthday party. In the short-term, Sally might feel better. After all, she doesn't have to socialise with all those people who will be there, nor does she have to worry about whether or not they like her or reject her. However, if she repeatedly cancels on parties and/or refuses invitations, she will also likely not be invited to parties in the future. In this sense, Sally's avoidance of going to the party created the very outcome she was trying to avoid – being alone.

Experiential avoidance typically does not give us an opportunity to learn that we are able to handle situations, which might scare and intimidate us. In fact, the more we avoid feared situations, the more likely we are to continue avoiding them, believing ourselves incapable of handling them. As a result, our world will become smaller and might not be entirely fulfilling.

Most strategies people use to feel better tend to fall under the 'experiential avoidance' definition. Is that the case for you? What have you tried in the past to better manage your difficult emotions or sensations? How did it turn out?

If you were able to find some patterns that normally work to help you manage your painful experiences without long-term detriment, great! They may be helpful. If not, then it might mean that these patterns are not helping you and you perhaps need to find another strategy.

The opposite of experiential avoidance is *acceptance* (the willingness to experience things that make us uncomfortable if it allows us to lead our lives in a more meaningful way). For example, if Passik, a fire-breathing dragon, is afraid of flying but really wants to see his dragon friend, Sam, he might be willing to experience the discomfort that comes with flying if that means that he gets to spend time with Sam.

Unfortunately, because you chose experiential avoidance you are stuck here, with the dark mists. The more you stab them, the more of them appear. Feel free to stay here as long as you'd like, but if you'd like to try something new, go to *page 89*.

Compassion Potion

Gain 3 inner strength points

Compassion refers to noticing the suffering of others and wanting to, or trying to, help them. Specifically, compassion consists of three elements:

1. Noticing that someone is struggling – for example, realising that Michael's anger is hurting him or noticing the extent of Katrina's shame.
2. Empathy – feeling the other person's emotion or trying to imagine how they feel with the understanding that most people struggle in a similar way. For example, realising that just like Michael, you too have felt angry and frustrated, and just like Katrina, you too have felt ashamed. Remembering what these emotions are like, or visually or emotionally connecting with the individual who is struggling, can help you to better understand how they feel, improving your empathic response.
3. The desire to help. This is crucial in a compassion response. In fact, when we feel like there is absolutely nothing we can do to help those who are struggling, we might be overwhelmed with something called *empathic distress,* where we only feel the pain of others but feel helpless to do anything about it. Empathic distress can make us feel overwhelmed with sadness, or anger at ourselves or the person who is struggling. On the other hand, offering to help the people who are struggling or (if it is not possible to offer your help directly), using the white magic of the Moon Tradition to send wishes of love and compassion

to those who are struggling, can often help soothe your own distress and might help the person who is struggling as well. (You will learn more about the Moon Tradition later on.)

In order to be effective at offering compassion to others, you need to also be able to offer compassion to yourself. This means that the three steps listed above need to apply to you as well. One of the ways that you might be able to help yourself when you see someone else struggling is to take three slow breaths, to allow yourself to become more settled and present, and then see if you can help others. Helping others can be beneficial not only for them, but for you as well. Helping other people can trigger the release of magical elements in our bodies, such as *oxytocin,* a hormone released when we hug or cuddle someone. Oxytocin is especially magical because it can help reduce our anxiety, depression and stress, and is suggested to increase lifespan.

Both Michael and Katrina seem to be struggling. Katrina seems to struggle with shame about her fear of heights, whereas Michael struggles with anger. There is no question that Michael acted in a hostile way, though understanding his emotions might help us better understand his behaviour. Anger is often thought of as a protective emotion, covering our *softer* emotion, such as sadness, fear, shame or insecurity. Anger can act as a scab for these softer emotions. It is possible that underneath Michael's anger is the fear that this mission will not succeed.

The best thing you can do in this situation is to consider what you need (a few breaths, for example, a walk, a time-out), as well as what Katrina and Michael need. Katrina most likely needs support and understanding. On the other hand, Michael might need your patience, as well as communication about how his actions are affecting you and others.

Continue to page 185.

Courage

Gain 3 courage points

Protecting others is very important to you and that means trying to support them as much as possible, even if you are scared. Sometimes following your core values, such as helping your friends, might bring on anxiety and fear. However, facing your fears in order to help others can actually allow you to find *courage*, an emotion that we feel when we are scared but are willing to face our fears.

In following Michael, you took a courageous step.

Proceed to page 62.

Trap

Lose 3 courage points

You choose to stay behind. Michael heads inside. There he learns an important clue of how to stop Mallena, but unfortunately, he is captured in the process. You see SAMs rushing inside; they arrest him and drag him away. You manage to hide but are unable to rescue him. He soon dies while imprisoned, the secret of defeating Mallena dying with him.

Mallena wins. You wake up in your bed. It's Monday. You are no longer Here. Here no longer exists.

The end.

<u>GO BACK TO THE BEGINNING AND TRY AGAIN.</u>

The Minotaurs shove all of you into a black vehicle. When they first approach the car, it does not seem large enough to fit a single Minotaur, let alone three of them, as well as an ogre and the rest of your group. However, much like Borreus' hut, you realise that it is much bigger on the inside, presumably by magic.

When all of you are inside and settled, the car drives off. Michael is still unconscious and is leaning against Gherk's shoulder. You look out the tinted windows. The car swerves down the mountain, as if on a bumpy carousel set at full speed. Trees, hills, roads seem as if they are flying past you.

'Uh-oh,' Lex says.

'What's wrong?' Talia asks.

'M-m-motion sickness,' Lex says. You realise the elf does look green and nauseated.

'Look straight ahead and focus on your breazing,' Anka says.

Lex does as instructed, breathing steadily until the car comes to a sudden stop that jolts Michael awake.

'Huh?' Michael asks as he sits up with a start, his left eye wide open, his right now purple and struggling to open, his fists clenched. You tense up too, watching his reaction.

'It's, uh, OK, Michael,' Gherk says.

Michael looks at Gherk, then takes a breath and looks around at all of you. Seeming to understand the situation, he unclenches his fists.

Some time between two minutes and an eternity later, the door opens.

'Out,' says Abbott, with disgust in his voice.

He pulls all of you out of the car, one by one, placing his hand on top of everyone's head to prevent it from being hit on the roof of the car. Gherk is the last to come out and, rather than protecting his head, Abbott shoves the ogre into the car.

'Oww!' Gherk screams as Michael turns and growls at Abbott.

'You really ought to watch where you put that ugly head of yours.' Abbott smirks. Capps sneers at his friend's remark.

'You watch it!' Michael snaps.

'Or what?' Capps says, getting into Michael's face. 'You want your left eye to match your right?'

'Enough!' Hoffman says in a stern voice.

'What? It's just an ogre.' Capps sniggers. 'You're not an ogre lover, are you, Sarge?'

'Shut up and bring them in,' Hoffman says, rolling his eyes. He then grabs Gherk by his shirt and escorts him inside, with your group following behind them, trailed by Capps and Abbott.

You all ascend stairs leading from the street to a tall, impressive building. In front of the entrance lobby stands a stone plaque that reads: *Magic Consulate Headquarters*.

Entering the lobby, the SAMs flash their identification badges at a Minotaur guard sitting behind an obsidian desk beside a large entryway. He is in the process of working out his crossword puzzle, a chewed pencil in his mouth.

'Just escorting the prisoners,' Hoffman explains.

'Mmm,' the entryway Minotaur grunts, without lifting his gaze from the puzzle.

The entryway leads you into a massive hallway lit with torches, candles and even several fireplaces. Pictures of nature – rainforests, waterfalls and beaches – line the walls of the consulate. Uniformed Minotaurs guard several other doors, though most of them do not appear to have much interest in their jobs. One of them, the one to the far right, is reading a book, titled: *Yoga 101: Embrace and Stretch your Inner Minotaur*. Two other SAMs are playing cards, while several others are placing bets on cat races. The cats do not seem to cooperate, hissing, purring or rubbing against the Minotaurs' legs.

'Amateurs,' you hear Hoffman mumble under his breath.

You are all led through a pair of large metal doors into what looks more like a small ballroom, with mirrored walls and decorated columns. Once all of you get in, Hoffman reaches to a control panel on the wall and presses a button marked *B*. The doors you just walked through close with a loud slam and the floor and walls rumble slightly. You realise you're in a massive lift on its way down. A minute later, when the lift doors open in what appears to be the basement, the scenery seems entirely different. Whereas the grand entry hallway above was warm, soothing and comfortable, the basement feels cold, with its plain white walls and overwhelming fluorescent lights.

'Let's go,' Hoffman says to your group. You all walk down the alarmingly bright hallway of bare walls with chipping paint. Sweet wrappers, empty drink bottles and pieces of old food are on the floor. Your shoes squish as you step on moist, gunky leftover food.

A tall, wide-bodied Minotaur walks down the hallway toward you. He is wearing several rank badges, though you are not sure what they all mean. When he gets closer, he stops and you can read his nametag: *Tyreck*.

'Hoffman!' Tyreck growls. 'I thought I told you to put the Krupinski file on my desk.'

Hoffman takes a slow breath before answering, visibly trying to control his temper. 'You asked me to put it in your mailbox, Chief, and that is in fact where I put it, sir.'

Tyreck huffs. 'Well, you need to *think* for a change, Hoffman! How the heck am I supposed to find it?'

'The mailbox is right next to your desk, sir. You had me put it there last month because you didn't want to walk to the mailbox room to get it, remember?'

'No,' Tyreck responds with a mocking tone.

Hoffman's eyes seem focused on one spot on the ground, his lips are pursed, his facial muscles are tensed; it is apparent that he is using every ounce of his willpower to keep his cool. He takes a few slow breaths before responding. 'Would you like me to take the file out of your mailbox and put it on your desk, sir?'

'What, do I have to do everything myself around here? Yes, I want you to put it on my desk.'

Hoffman sighs, pursing his lips tighter.

'Now, Hoffman!'

'Yes, sir,' Hoffman manages to say through gritted teeth. He heads in the direction from which Tyreck came.

'Oh, by the way, Hoffman,' Tyreck calls to him.

Hoffman stops and turns around. 'Sir?'

'Your wife called. She's in the hospital again.'

Hoffman's face falls as Tyreck laughs. 'I guess you should stop hitting her.'

You notice Hoffman squeezing his hands into tight fists. 'My wife has cancer, sir.'

'Oh, lighten up, Dayton. It's just a joke.'

With what you expect is his last ounce of patience, Hoffman says, 'With all due respect, sir, domestic violence isn't something to joke about. And neither is cancer. *Sir.*'

'Oh, blah!' Tyreck waves at him dismissively and walks away without any interest in the prisoners.

Hoffman growls and storms off.

'What should we do with them?' asks Abbott, pointing to all of you.

Capps shrugs. 'No idea. Should we ask Tyreck?'

'Nah. Better not. He usually knows less than we do.'

'Interrogations rooms?' Capps asks him.

'Sure, why not?'

The SAMs push you all down the revolting corridor, which now smells of stale water and rotten eggs. They turn the corner toward a wall of locked doors and shove each of you into separate rooms. The room you're in is small and dank, smelling like an old rubbish bin. Fluorescent light bulbs flicker at an insufferable rate. It looks like at some point there were several layers of wallpaper here, now long gone and leaving barely visible patches. The rest of the walls look like someone made a frequent sport of throwing food against them. There is a table in the middle of the room, the surface occupied by an abundance of fast-moving ants that busily consume nearby crumbs and dead roaches.

Your stomach turns at this repulsive sight.

If you choose to turn away from the cockroaches and ignore the disgusting display, turn to page 107.

If you choose to face it, turn to page 6.

You walk in after Michael, so closely behind, in fact, that you almost expect to knock into him when he stops in his tracks. But to your surprise he is now already standing at the other end of the cottage's living room. This peculiar little building that stands on chicken legs appears to be much larger on the inside than it seems on the outside. The bare walls and the few pieces of furniture – including a shabby table and three rusty chairs – are all grey and pallid.

The rest of the legion follows you in and shares your surprise.

'Whoa!' you say. 'It's huge.'

'It's enchanted to bend the laws of physics,' Celeste explains.

'You can do that?' you ask.

'If you know the right spell.'

'Who's there?' an old squeaky voice comes from another room.

There is a sound of shuffling feet and an old grey-haired, grey-bearded, grey-skinned man, wearing a grey robe, walks into the living room. He is hunched over. He gazes down at the floor, pants and groans as he walks, each step apparently causing excruciating pain. He leans on an ancient, grey staff with a large, hoary crystal at the top of it.

Seeing all of you, he points his staff at your group and yells, his speech fast and pressured: 'Who are you? What are you doing here? Have you come to steal my sazaár? Well, I sold it and the guy gave me two thousand gold coins for it, but they were all fake anyway, they just happened to be chocolate coins, and I ate them, so you can't have them!'

'Excuse me, sir?' you say. He looks at you, bewildered. 'Are you by any chance Borreus the Warlock?'

'Who wants to know? You think you can—'

'We are trying to stop—'

'—just kill me?'

'—Mallena from destroying the—'

'Wait – *what*?'

'*What*?'

You look at each other in confusion. Then, the old warlock plops himself onto the closer of the two chairs. He sighs, rubbing his swollen wrists as he speaks again.

'Arthritis, you know? Hard to do any spells with arthritis. The irony is that the anti-inflammatory spell requires your hands and I can't . . . well.'

'Here. Allow me,' Celeste says.

The man looks up curiously as she takes a chug from her coffee mug, puts it on the table, and then walks over to him, gesturing that she'd like to take his right wrist. He nods and Celeste gently takes hold with both of her hands before closing her eyes, taking a breath and speaking her spell. A pale circle of silvery-purple light surrounds them, casting a welcome change on to the grey room. She then takes the man's other wrist and repeats the enchantment. You can see the relief in the old warlock's face when she lets go, and you can see that the wrists are no longer swollen.

'Thank you, child,' Borreus says, his voice now slower and more humble. 'Now, what can I do for you?'

'We know that Mallena recently came to see you and we were hoping that you could tell us why,' you say.

The man looks up at you suspiciously. 'Why?'

'She's trying to control people's emotions and it's causing cata-strophic effects,' Michael says. 'We were told you helped her numb her own emotions. Is that true?'

'Yes,' the old warlock says softly, lowering his head. 'I did.'

'Can you please tell us how?' Lex asks.

'The choker . . .' he says in a whisper, looking off into the distance. A little louder, he clarifies, 'The choker. The choker, you see? The Painless Choker.'

All of you exchange glances as the man, now more animated, launches into a rapid explanation, without pause for a breath. 'People kill for it and people crave it, they think it will give them relief but it won't, it's like I told my wife, Neela, when she was alive – turning off painful emotions also turns off joy, happiness, your whole reason for living, people think they would be better off not feeling their painful emotions but the pain of numbness hurts so much more, it's like being stabbed a thousand times through the heart and not caring, because the pain is so bad that you begin to feel nothing at all, it's like I told Neela – that's my wife – when we were in Norway and she wanted to buy the yellow shoes but I thought that she—'

'Excuse me, Mr Borreus?' Lex says timidly. 'I'm so sorry to interrupt you, sir. This choker – how is it connected with her power?'

The old warlock looks at Lex and then your entire group. 'You lot. You weren't kidding. You really think you can stop Mallena from spreading her control over Here?'

'Well, at the very least, we need to try,' Michael says, determined. 'Can you help us?'

Borreus' face is now as grey as his robes, his face almost entirely ashen. He leans in closer to Michael, as if checking for spies. 'You have to remove the choker from her neck and destroy it. This will take away her power. But you must do it before it destroys you, before it takes away the very thing you love the most, before it—'

'How? How do we destroy it?' Michael interrupts.

'Let me see,' the old man says, getting up with a groan. He supports his spine with his left hand, holding his staff in his right, and slowly shuffles out of the room, adding on his way out, 'Help yourself to some sweets.'

Your stomach growls as you look at the large bowl filled with sweets of different sizes, all individually wrapped in silver-grey wrappers. You approach and unwrap a grey-coloured sweet that reminds you of chocolate. You put it in your mouth, salivating as you expect to taste a familiar chocolaty flavour. However, it does not taste like chocolate. It does not taste like anything at all. It tastes . . . empty.

You turn to Anka to ask her about this but the old man re-emerges, shuffling out from his bedroom. Suddenly he stops, looking at all of you, evidently scared and confused.

'Who are you?' he finally asks, pointing his staff at all of you again, his face looking even greyer than before.

'Please, Mr Borreus. We just met a few minutes ago. You were going to tell us how to destroy the Painless Choker.'

'The what, now?' he asks. His eyelids look heavy, his gaze is unfocused, and his skin is nearly transparent.

There is a knock on the door.

'Who's there?' the old man calls out, without moving his body.

'Special Agents of Magic. Open up!'

SAMs!

Panic ignites in yourself and the others. Michael places himself between the legion and the door, assuming a fighting pose, while Celeste whispers to Java, 'Warn Katrina!'

Java nods and launches out the open window just as the front door is kicked in with a loud thud, and then it squeaks, barely hanging on its hinges.

Special Agent Hoffman and the other two Minotaurs, Abbott and Capps, enter. They look even more aggressive than before, their eyebrows furrowed, their bodies exuding hostility.

'Thanks for the tip, Borreus,' Hoffman says. 'We'll take it from here.'

The old man does not answer. He looks frozen, the light from his eyes slowly going out right in front of you.

'Borreus? Borreus? Are you OK?' you ask him.

He does not answer.

Anka approaches him. 'Are you OK?' she asks, shaking his shoulders. 'Do you need—?'

The old warlock's collar pops open and around his neck you see a thin silver choker with a blinking red light. Anka gasps and lets go of Borreus as he slowly fades away, and then, seconds later, vanishes completely, his cottage leaving with him. You and the legion are left standing by the swamp with Hoffman and the other SAMs.

'Where did he go?' you ask, your voice shaking.

'Who?' asks Abbott.

'Borreus. The old warlock!'

'Who?' Capps asks.

You exchange worried looks with the others. Talia looks furious. 'He was just here. He was here and he disappeared, just like the others have, and nobody cares!'

'Who disappeared?' Hoffman asks. 'Are you reporting a missing person?'

'YES!' She shouts at him. 'Yes! Borreus! He disappeared right in front of your eyes! Why can't you remember him?'

'I remember him,' Michael says. 'He was a traitor and got what he deserved.'

'He was still a person!' you snap, shocked at his apathy. Something at the very core of you begins to hurt.

'All right, enough!' Hoffman shouts. 'You are all under arrest. You need to come with us.'

'On what charge?' Michael asks.

'Treason. Specifically, conspiring to assassinate the Head of the Magic Consulate, Mallena Phobian.'

'WHAT?' you, Michael and Talia shout at once.

'Let's go!' Capps shouts.

Michael steps forward. 'You are going to have to take us by force.'

'Gladly.' Capps smirks and hits Michael on the face with his giant club, knocking him to the ground.

Michael hits his head on a boulder and stops moving. You and the rest of your group gasp. Capps raises his club to hit Michael again but Gherk runs toward him and blocks Michael with his body. He screams in pain as the club hits his shoulder but he does not move.

'Get out of the way, stupid ogre!' Capps shouts.

'Uh, no,' Gherk says, rubbing his shoulder.

'Have it your way.' Capps raises his club again and delivers several blows to the ogre's face, arms and back.

'ENOUGH!' shouts Hoffman. 'There is no need to use excessive force!' He then turns to you and the rest of the legion. 'Come with us. Peacefully, please. There's no need for anyone else to get hurt.'

You sigh and join Talia, Anka and Lex in following Hoffman toward his car. Gherk carefully lifts Michael's unmoving body and follows as well, Capps and Abbott walking behind them, playing with their clubs with menace in their eyes.

Turn to page 57.

Mindfulness Spell

Gain 3 wisdom points

You are HERE.

Take a slow breath. Notice the sensation of the breath in your chest and stomach as you breathe in and as you breathe out. Notice the sensations of your feet. Notice that at this very moment, you are Here. In this moment, the world hasn't ended.

Simply noticing your breath, or the sensation of your feet making contact with the ground, noticing your emotions, thoughts or sensations, are all a part of the *Mindfulness Spell.* Mindfulness means paying attention to the present moment. This magical spell allows you to notice what you are experiencing at *this moment*, as opposed to what you are afraid of feeling in the future or have felt in the past.

A mindful activity can be anything – brushing your teeth, petting your cat, taking a shower, eating, drinking tea or coffee, or doing the dishes. Simply noticing your sensations is a part of mindfulness.

Mindfulness does not mean that you need to have an empty mind. It is not actually possible to be free of thoughts for an extended period of time. Mindfulness simply means noticing, which includes noticing that you might have become distracted, and then bringing your attention back to your task.

So, at this moment, bring your attention to your breathing, and notice the sensation of your feet or arms.

Then proceed to page 49.

Your eyelids feel as if they are weighted down. Your nose has grown accustomed to the smell, and the table and its inhabitants no longer bother you. You find yourself wishing you were still at home in your bed and wonder if you'll ever be able to return home again. You fight to keep your eyes open but finally you can't.

The sound of keys jingling in the lock wakes you, followed by voices outside. The door opens and Hoffman walks in, accompanied by a thin woman with dark wavy hair, wearing a red corseted dress with black stripes. Her eyes are the colour of fresh grass and her bow-shaped lips match the scarlet shade of her dress. Around her neck is a thin silver choker.

She smiles at you, showing off her perfectly straight, pearly white teeth. Her tone is sweet but her vulturine presence feels unsettling. 'Hello. My name is Mallena Phobian. And you are?'

As you try to regain your breath and introduce yourself to the very sorceress you're somehow supposed to defeat, she walks toward you, only to then stop and look at the bug-infested table. Raising her hands, she makes a quick sequenced move, like a maestro directing an orchestra, and the insects disappear. A few more coordinated movements from her and the table is covered with a fresh white cloth that materialises from the air. A few more gestures and the table now holds hot breads, soft cheeses, fresh meats, salads, fruits and mouth-watering pastries. Your mouth salivates and you swallow, your growling stomach a clear indication of your ravenous state.

'Please, my dear, eat. You must be starving. You've been cooped up in this . . . *room* for over eighteen hours now,' the sorceress says.

Eighteen hours?!

'Please,' she says again, pointing to the food. 'Eat.'

You look at her and then at Hoffman, unsure of what you should do.

'Oh, for crying out loud! It's not poisoned!' Mallena exclaims, and takes a bite of the chicken and eats one of the pastries. 'See? All good. Now, dig in.'

She doesn't look poisoned. You approach cautiously and take a small bite of one of the pastries. Your stomach gives an appreciative rumble. Each bite fills you with warmth and delicious goodness. You are not sure if this is truly the most delicious meal you've ever had or if you're just the most starved you've ever been. Either way, the food tastes amazing.

When you are finally finished, you sit back and sigh, feeling full. Your comfort is short-lived, though, as once again the sorceress approaches you.

'You must have been starving,' Mallena says, smiling her pearly-whites at you. 'That's quite the journey you and your friends took. My sources tell me that you visited Serena at the Black Lake before going all the way to see Borreus. Is that true?'

You say nothing.

'Don't worry. You don't have to say anything. I'm not Here to interrogate you. I just wanted to be a gracious host. I understand that you are the Chosen One. Tell me, dear, how is it that you plan to defeat me?' Her face no longer looks sweet. Instead she looks numb and stern.

Still you say nothing.

'Tell me,' she continues, leaning in over you, 'what is so special about you that makes you, and only *you* of all people, the Chosen One?'

'NOTHING!' a voice in your head says. It sounds as if it is coming through a pair of headphones, a message transmitted

directly into your head, one you cannot turn off. '*There is nothing special about you. NOTHING!*'

'What . . . what did you . . . give me?' you finally manage to get out.

'Nothing that you didn't already have.' She smirks. 'The potion merely magnifies it.'

'Potion?'

'The Fusion Potion, yes. It makes your thoughts fuse with your biggest insecurities and makes you accept them as if they were facts.'

As she speaks, the voice in your head continues to torment you. '*You are such an idiot! You should have known not to eat anything she gave you! You are such a moron! You are going to fail! You have no idea what you're doing!*'

'Stop!' you try to shout at the voice, but your words are stifled.

'*You can't stop me. I live inside you. I see to the very depth of you and I see how useless and pathetic you are.*'

'Stop it!' you try to shout out again, but it's useless.

'*No one loves you. No one needs you. No one cares about you. So why don't you just give up and kill yourself already?*'

A familiar tidal wave of depression washes over you. Your body is heavy and yet empty at the same time. Everything hurts but also everything is numb. It feels . . . hopeless. You try to shut it out. All of it. The emotions. The thoughts. But similar to the hydra-like Strah, these painful thoughts multiply. The excruciating emotions – depression, shame, fear, and the horrifying thoughts – get so intense that you cover your ears to try to block them out. But they only grow louder.

Mallena laughs. 'Don't be ridiculous. There's no escaping your thoughts and feelings. In fact, the more you try to fight these, the stronger they get. Face it, you're stuck.'

You are now doubling over from emotional pain. It is the most agonising thing you've ever felt in your entire life.

'P-p-p-please,' you plead. 'Make . . . it . . . stop.'

'My pleasure,' she says with a malicious smile and a glint in her eyes. 'Here you go.' She slides a thin silver choker across the table to you. It looks just like the one she's wearing. 'Put that on until it clicks. The little red light will turn on when it is activated. This will take away all your pain. For ever.'

'The P-p-painless Ch-Choker?' you stutter.

'Ah, Borreus *did* tell you. It takes away your ability to feel physical and emotional pain. It's quite brilliant, really.'

'It killed him,' you say, starting to feel angry and a little braver, despite the loud voices in your mind.

'No, no, no, my dear,' she says with a tone of condescension. 'Borreus was old. It was his time, I'm afraid. That is something no choker or magical artefact can prevent.'

'What about all those other people who disappeared?' you ask.

'People who disappear do so because of the deep and intense emotional pain that they are in. The Painless Choker allows them to improve the quality of their lives.'

You look at her. She doesn't seem to be disappearing. Or scared. Or sick. Or hurt in any way. She is wearing the choker. She said it could take all your pain away. *But is it worth it?*

'The choker can take away all my pain?' you ask.

'Yes. All of it. Leaving you to live out your life without any pain. Without any hurt. No fear. No depression. No anxiety ever again. Don't you want that?'

'Of course I do,' you snap, noticing your heart pounding again.

Do it! You are pathetic! Do you want to be the pathetic loser that you are for ever? Do you want to be the coward that you are for the rest of your life? Do it! Take it! Wear it!'

'Go ahead. Try it on,' Mallena says, handing the choker to you.

Proceed to page 122.

Disconnection Fusion

Lose all your points

You put on the Painless Choker and immediately feel relieved. The voices stop and you no longer feel afraid, depressed or scared. You do not feel ashamed, insecure or embarrassed. You are no longer concerned about what happens to the other members of the legion or if they're safe. You don't feel anxious about what you're supposed to do or if you'll ever get back home. You do not feel joy, love or connection.

You are empty.

Escaping the painful emotions causes you to numb all of them, including ones you want to feel. Life feels bland, meaningless and grey. There doesn't seem to be any point to continuing your mission, so you give up. Mallena wins.

The end.

GO BACK TO THE BEGINNING AND TRY AGAIN.

You look at Celeste. 'I don't know what I'm doing. I have a group of strangers suddenly relying on me and I'm supposed to defeat someone that I don't know anything about in a world I don't understand. I'm terrified that I'm not good enough at anything to help you, that I'll fail you all, and that soon enough you'll all hate me, and—'

'Look!' Celeste shouts as she points to your arm. There, exactly where she is pointing, is now a small dark balloon mark with the words *You are HERE* written underneath it.

'I need to see everyone's MESS marks,' Hoffman demands as everyone unfreezes.

Celeste collapses to the floor. Katrina rushes over to help her.

'What's wrong with her?' Hoffman asks.

'Fainted, I'm afraid,' Katrina responds. 'It happens to her sometimes. Burnout, you know?'

'Right. Well, your arms, please,' Hoffman says as Gherk carries Celeste to the couch and Katrina follows to help.

Hoffman inspects everyone's marks, gruffly and quickly, as Capps and Abbott keep guard. When he approaches Michael, he reaches for his arm.

'You must be joking,' Michael snaps.

'You know the rules, Ellison.'

'But you know me.'

'Rules are rules.'

Michael curses under his breath but doesn't argue any more. Hoffman inspects his arm and seems satisfied. Then he checks Celeste's arm as she begins to reawaken. Finally, the Minotaur approaches you. As he takes your arm, you tense up from his harsh touch. As he's rolling up your sleeve his phone rings.

'Excuse me,' he says as he picks up the phone and walks a few feet away from you. 'Hello? . . . Oh, hello, sweetheart.' His voice lowers slightly, but you can tell his brusque tone is gentler now. 'No, I'm sorry, I don't . . . No, I don't know when I'll be home . . . Of course, I can stop by the pharmacy . . . You got it. I have to . . . I have to go now . . . I know, sweetie, but . . . I know . . . I'm working, honey . . . I miss you too. Bye.'

His eyes look red and heavy. He walks up to you and inspects your arm. You notice that everyone is staring, as if still under Celeste's spell.

'This seems new,' Hoffman says with suspicion in his voice. 'When did you get Here?'

You freeze, unsure how to respond. You once again wonder if you've made the right decision and wait for everyone to realise that you are a fraud.

'Just today,' you finally muster. 'I—'

Hoffman's phone rings again. Hoffman checks the caller ID and visibly tenses.

'It's Tyreck,' he says to the other Minotaurs, with the tone of someone about to clean a clogged toilet. He sighs and answers the phone. 'Hello, Chief . . . Yes, sir . . . No, sir, we are just checking on . . . Yes, sir, I left them on your desk, as you requested . . . No, sir, I don't know who took your cookies . . . No, sir, I did not eat them . . . No, sir, I don't think Abbott or Capps ate them either . . . I don't need to ask them, sir, I've been with them all day . . .' He sighs and shakes his head. 'Yes, sir.'

Hoffman then turns to the other two Minotaurs. 'The chief wants to know if either of you ate his cookies.'

Abbott and Capps shake their heads begrudgingly. Hoffman sighs again and then addresses his caller.

'No, sir, they did not . . . What? Right now? . . . OK . . . OK . . . We are on our way.' Hanging up the phone with an irritated sigh, Hoffman turns to his colleagues. 'Let's go.'

And with that the Minotaurs leave. You can hardly believe your luck.

'Well,' says Michael, pointing to your mark, his tone noticeably softer than before. 'Looks like you belong Here after all.'

Your cheeks blush and your mouth widens into a smile.

Continue to page 32.

Defusion Potion

Gain 5 courage points

The Fusion Potion is hard to beat. It gets into your mind like an evil virus, making you believe that the harrowing thoughts you are experiencing are actually facts. This isn't true, of course. Our thoughts aren't necessarily facts. And this is where we can use a nifty antidote, the *Defusion Potion**.

The Defusion Potion is one of the hardest potions to make because the ingredients of it are all in your mind. It takes a great deal of concentration and practice.

Ready?

The most crucial step to preparing this antidote is to mindfully acknowledge that you are having a particular thought. For example, rather than saying, 'I am a failure,' you can say, 'I am having the thought that I am a failure.' This practice creates some distance between you and the thought, thus reducing your *fusion* with it. If you are able to see it as a thought, one of many thoughts that go through our minds, no different than any silly thought, such as 'I am a banana', it will reduce some of the hold that this thought has on you.

The next step to making the Defusion Potion is to purposely recite the demonising thought over and over and over again out loud. For example: 'I'm having a thought that I'm a failure, I'm having a thought that I'm a failure, I'm having a thought that I'm a failure . . .' Try saying that out loud for two minutes.

What did you notice? As the antidote begins to work, it reduces the meaning of the harsh words. In fact, as you repeat the words, they begin to blend together into meaningless sounds.

As with any recipe, the Defusion Potion can be prepared in other ways as well. For example, you might also benefit from recognising the Fusion Potion as just one of Mallena's many attempts to hold you back from what is really important to you. In response, you can practise saying something along the lines of: 'I know what you're trying to do. But it will not work. Your spell might be powerful but my mission is too important to be held back by you.'

Take your time to prepare and process this antidote, whichever way you choose to prepare it.

*Note that this antidote may not take away your thoughts and feelings. However, the goal is to reduce the *fusion,* or the hold that the initial potion had on you.

Once you are ready to continue, proceed to page 163.

'Oh, no! No, no, no!' Lex screams, shaking Talia. 'Talia. Talia, c'mon, wake up.'

Talia blinks her eyes open. Her eyes, previously reddish-brown, are now a bluish shade of grey. They look icy and unfocused.

'Talia, why?' Lex asks through tears.

'Why what?' Talia asks flatly.

'Why did you put on the choker?'

'It just made sense to do it,' Talia responds, no emotion in her voice. 'I was suffering. Now I'm not.'

'I ... I ... just don't ... You'll die,' Lex whispers. 'You'll disappear.'

Lex reaches out to hold Talia's hand, but she pulls it away. Lex stands up slowly, trembling, and walks off to the other end of the cell, burying their head in their arms.

'Is there anything we can do?' you ask Anka.

'I do not know,' she says remorsefully. 'I do not know if zere actually is a vay to remove ze choker. I sink ze only sing ve can do now is—'

She's cut short by the sound of fairy dust, sounding like gentle winter chimes. All of you turn to see a petite purple-winged fairy standing just outside the jail cell. She looks to be about two feet high. Tattoos of lilies, lotus flowers and Gaelic symbols cover her limbs, and her black and purple dress perfectly matches the colours of her long, straight hair. She wears a thin gold necklace, decorated by a golden crescent of the moon with a red heart in the centre.

'Stand back,' she says in a low but firm voice.

You all comply as she reaches into the pocket of her dress and pulls out a handful of golden fairy dust. She throws it at the cell bars and they instantly disappear.

'Name's Eribelle. Follow me. Now,' she says matter-of-factly.

'We are not going anywhere,' Michael says. 'This could be another trap.'

The fairy scoffs. 'Enough dilly-dallying! Java sent me to help get you all out. Now, let's go! Go! GO! This enchantment won't hold for ever!'

You exchange looks with the others and nod. You follow Eribelle out. Michael walks behind you, seemingly intent on protecting you. Gherk carries Celeste, who is still unconscious. Lex leads Talia by the hand, a blank expression on her once-animated face. Anka keeps guard at the very back.

You follow Eribelle down the same filthy hallway you walked before. You find four Minotaurs there, who have all been knocked out.

'Your doing?' Michael asks Eribelle, impressed.

'No, that was the tooth fairy,' she responds sarcastically. 'Keep moving.'

You continue down the corridor when Eribelle stops so abruptly that you almost knock her over. She turns to you and puts one finger to her mouth to indicate for all of you to keep silent. You hear approaching stomping footsteps. It sounds like at least a couple of Minotaurs are marching down the parallel hallway.

'. . . and then I told him that I don't want no ogres around,' you hear one of them say.

'Ogres,' another one scoffs. 'Should be skinned. Each and every one of them. And don't even get me started on werewolves.'

The first one responds, 'I've been saying that we should just kick them all out to the woods. Build a fence. Keep them out.'

'My ex actually married one of them. An ogre. Disgusting race . . .'

You look over to Gherk and see his face. His nose and lips tremble slightly. In so many ways he is just like you, someone who just wants to be accepted, and loved. As all beings do.

You wish you could say something. Something to them, to stop them from being so horrible. To him, to assure him that he is not alone, to not listen to those awful things that the Minotaurs say about him and his kind. Instead, you put your hand on Gherk's arm and look into his eyes, hoping that your look tells him: 'I know this is hard. I see you. You are loved.'

Gherk smiles appreciatively and sniffles.

'What's that?' the first Minotaur asks.

'I didn't hear anything.'

'Better check it out.'

You tense up and turn to look at your group. Michael assumes a fighting position while Lex reaches for the arrows in the quiver.

As the first Minotaur emerges from around the corner, Eribelle throws a handful of fairy dust at him, shouting, 'Gelér!'

The Minotaur's face grows stiff with shock and he collapses on the ground.

'There's someone there!' shouts one of the Minotaurs. 'Sound the alarm.'

'Run!' Eribelle shouts, and all of you follow her, the sound of the alarm blaring and flashing lights nearly blinding you.

'Stop!' one of the Minotaurs yells at your group. And then to the SAMs, 'It's the prisoners!'

'I got one!' one of the SAMs exclaims as he grabs Talia, who appears too numb to fight back.

Lex fires an arrow at his foot. The Minotaur yelps and lets go of Talia. Lex drags her away.

'Stop! Special Agents of Magic!' another Minotaur shouts. 'I said, STOP!'

You all run as fast as you can, until a swarm of SAMs cuts you off.

'Stop. Please. We don't want to hurt you,' says the Minotaur closest to you, whose nametag reads: Kasper.

'Except that ogre,' the SAM next to him says. 'He's going to—'

'Shut it, Braxbane!' Kasper snaps at him. 'There's enough of that going on around the world. We need to be uniting, not—'

'Oh, spare me your flower power, Kas,' Braxbane says.

'Enough!' Kasper snaps again and then turns to the group. 'I apologise for my colleague's behaviour but I'm afraid you're going to have to come with us.'

'Clôture!' Eribelle shouts, throwing handfuls of fairy dust in front of and behind your group.

A wooden fence appears between you and the Minotaurs.

'Portail!' she shouts again, throwing golden dust at the wall. A portal opens, leading out to the woods.

'Come on!' she yells. 'We only have thirty seconds before these wear off.'

She goes through and the rest of you follow. Michael helps Lex drag Talia through the portal, while Gherk carries Celeste as if she were a feather. You leave last as the Minotaurs knock the fence down. You turn back in time to see the portal closing as the bewildered SAMs are looking through it.

'Follow me!' Eribelle yells. 'Hurry!'

You take off after the fairy, her body glowing with purple light in the dark forest as you hear the Minotaurs shouting in the darkness. They can't be too far away. You follow Eribelle's illuminating light, but cannot see where you are going, bumping into bushes and trees. Your face and limbs are full of scratches and bug bites by the time you arrive at the base of a tall maple tree. A tree house above you is nestled between it and another maple tree. Eribelle stops, feels in between the branches and pulls out an end of a rope secured at the base of the house.

'Eribelle?' a familiar voice calls out.

'Java!' you exclaim excitedly as the raven emerges from the bushes and flies toward Gherk, who still holds Celeste's unconscious body.

'What happened to her?' the raven asks.

'She, uh, did, uh, a spell to, uh, help us and, uh—'

'I think I get the picture,' Java replies.

'This way,' Eribelle says, quickly pulling herself up the rope. When she reaches the top, she looks back down to all of you. 'Hurry!'

Gherk gently places Celeste over his left shoulder and climbs up.

'C'mon, Talia. I need you to climb,' Lex says, gently shaking her shoulder. 'C'mon. Please.'

Talia stares blankly into the distance and doesn't move. Lex tries but is unable to hold Talia and simultaneously pull them both up the rope.

'Vait,' says Anka. 'Ve vill tie her up and Gherk vill pull.'

Anka and Lex tie the rope around Talia's arms and waist, creating a harness. At Lex's signal, the ogre lifts up Talia into the tree house. Throughout it all, Talia doesn't struggle, remaining immobile and silent.

After the rope is sent back down, Lex climbs up and then Anka, leaving only you and Michael. He helps you lift yourself up and you slowly begin to climb – not an easy task. Halfway up, your shoulders, biceps and triceps feel like they're tearing. By the time you reach the top, your neck is so stiff, you're unsure you'll ever turn your head in either direction again. Gherk and Anka help you up as Michael climbs up after you. When he arrives, Eribelle pulls up the rope and closes the door.

Once you're able to catch your breath and stretch a bit, you take a look around. The ceiling is almost low enough to reach without standing on your tiptoes. Gherk has to sit down on the floor so as not to bump his head. A tiny fireplace keeps the room lit and warm, though its twinkling purple flames suggest that it's run off fairy dust, so as not to burn the tree down. Several purple and golden shimmering candles glow with the same kind of fairy dust, adding to the room's ambience. Celeste is resting on one of the two couches as Java sits next to her head.

'Sit,' Eribelle says, pointing to a small brown couch behind you.

You sit on one end, relieved at being able to rest on soft, comfortable cushions as you notice the immense soreness of your muscles. You realise how much you've been neglecting your body. You haven't been eating enough or sleeping enough. You actually miss the boring days when you weren't running away from homicidal sorcerers who intended to start the apocalypse.

Celeste rolls onto her side and sits up slowly. She groggily asks, 'Umm . . . what happened? Where's Java?'

'Shhh,' Java says in a soothing voice, perching beside her. 'Lie down. We are safe.'

Celeste lies back down, looking pale and worn.

'That was a powerful potion you all took,' Eribelle remarks. 'It's no wonder that Celeste was weakened. First order of business, we need to make sure you all heal. I will teach you elements of white magic to withstand the Fusion Potion and other difficulties you might face.'

'What about Talia?' Lex asks. 'Is she going to die?'

'I don't know,' Eribelle responds. 'But our primary focus needs to be on healing all of you first.'

'There's no time!' Lex shouts. 'We have to do something! Do you not understand that we are losing her every minute?'

Eribelle's face softens. She walks over to Lex and takes the elf's hands into hers. 'Lex, I know that you are worried about her. And believe me, the best way we can help her is to first give yourself and all of us the strength that we need to be able to combine our efforts to break the curse of the choker. If you try to help her while you are struggling, you will only burn yourself out and will most likely not be able to help. So, if you want to help her, you need to heal yourself first.'

Lex exhales, seemingly frustrated, but does not argue.

Eribelle walks over to the tiny window and turns to face everyone. 'To help you begin to recover from the Fusion Potion, as well as cope with some obstacles you are likely to face, I am going to teach you the Moon Tradition.'

'Yes, Serena mentioned it to us vhen ve visited her,' Anka says. 'Vhat is ze Moon Tradition?'

Eribelle points to the golden crescent necklace she wears. 'The love-filled moon is its symbol. The Moon Tradition uses the ultimate white magic of love and compassion for oneself and others, healing the effects and injuries of dark magic.'

Lex seems infuriated, but remains quiet.

Michael scoffs, 'We have only a matter of days to stop that bitch! We need to storm the castle, not sing Kumbaya in the middle of the woods!'

'No, Eribelle is right,' Lex says, exhaling. 'We don't even know how to destroy the choker yet. We can't afford to just barge in there like a bunch of savages!'

Michael goes red in the face. 'Who are you calling a savage, Elf?'

'What is that supposed to mean?'

'Stop,' Eribelle says in a firm voice. 'This is not you talking. The aggression and anger you're experiencing, these are the effects of the Fusion Potion. We need to practise the Moon Tradition before it gets any worse and you wind up begging Mallena for the choker.'

Michael turns to face you. 'Well? What do you say we should do?'

Everyone else turns to you as well. You gulp, realising that you have to make a decision.

If you choose to stay and practise the Moon Tradition, go to page 25.

If you choose to leave and head toward Mallena's castle, go to page 149.

Acceptance Spell

Gain 4 courage points

You put down the knife. You're afraid, yes, but for a moment you pretend that you're not. You stand up straight and face the monsters. They pause and you can feel your voice come back as you say, 'I'm here. You're here. You're not going away? Fine. Neither am I.'

The mist creatures continue to float around you but don't move. You have accidentally managed to cast the Acceptance Spell, a magical spell, like the type that witches and wizards use in fantasy films and comics. The creatures back away slightly, as if afraid of you, now that you have learned this new spell.

Facing your monsters is never easy. However, running away from your emotional monsters is analogous to chopping off a head of a hydra – once you cut off one head, two more grow in its place.

Neither running away from these monsters nor trying to force them away is working, so you need to find another, more adaptive solution. One coping strategy is *acceptance*. Acceptance is the willingness to experience your difficult internal sensations. Using the Acceptance Spell does not mean that you have to like your painful emotions, nor does it ever mean that whatever painful experience happened to you was OK. Rather, it means: *accepting that you are feeling the way you are feeling and accepting that the situation did occur.*

Acceptance is a very advanced form of magic and we will be returning to it later in the book, so don't worry if you are unsure about whether you want to try it. *In the meantime, if you are willing to try a different strategy for facing the smoke-breathing dark mists, go to page 159.*

Go to Sleep

Lose 4 courage points

Anka leaves and you go back to your room. You fall asleep and wake up again, running behind schedule but satisfied that the monsters were a strange dream. You go on living your life in the real world, where mist monsters only exist in books like this one. It seems safer. But you can't stop wondering what would have happened if you'd said yes to joining a real quest. If only you could go back and say yes. If only . . .

YOUR QUEST ENDS HERE, BUT DO RETURN TO THE START AND SEE IF THERE ARE OTHER CHOICES YOU COULD MAKE.

'To start,' Eribelle says, touching her necklace, 'I'd like you all to sit comfortably.'

'This is such a waste of time,' Michael mutters as he sits next to you. 'I hope you know what you are doing.'

You say nothing, knowing that, once again, you don't.

'The practice consists of three steps – Mindful Defusion, Common Humanity, and Loving Kindness to yourself and others.'

Michael sighs, rolling his eyes. 'This is so ridiculous.'

Eribelle smiles at him, kindness gleaming in her hazel eyes. 'Sometimes resistance indicates that we are struggling.'

'What do you mean?' Michael asks.

'When we struggle with any painful emotions, such as fear, insecurity, anxiety or shame, or when we experience chronic physical pain, we might be resistant to any activity, which has any chance of bringing up these painful sensations. The Moon Tradition teaches us to identify these experiences and label them, to recognise that we are not alone in this struggle, and to find a way to practise kindness and soothing, for ourselves and for others. We will start with the first step – *Mindful Defusion*. To practise it, take a few moments to identify your thoughts and feelings out loud, labelling them as thoughts and feelings. For example, for me, I am having a thought . . . that I am an amateur and not a good enough Moon Tradition teacher. And I am having a feeling of . . . insecurity, anxiety and self-doubt.'

You are surprised to hear Eribelle's self-doubting thoughts. *She appears so confident!* You take a breath and focus in on your own thoughts and feelings.

'I'm having a sought zat I am a fraud,' Anka says out loud.

You look up at her, surprised. Her thought is identical to yours. It feels strangely comforting to know that you are not alone in thinking this way.

'I'm having a thought that if I don't help enough people, that means I am worthless,' Celeste says.

'I'm having a thought that I am a failure in every way,' Lex says.

Gherk lowers his head as he says, 'I, uh, am having the thought that, uh, I am, uh, worthless, stupid and, uh, a disappointment. I, uh, feel ashamed and, uh, sad.'

'I'm having a thought that I am a fraud . . . and that I will let you all down,' you finally say. 'I am . . . feeling anxious, scared and ashamed.'

Everyone looks at you. You blush, immediately regretting sharing your thoughts and feelings.

Michael studies you in surprise. 'I never would have known that you are struggling too. You seem so confident. Me, I struggle all the time. I'm . . . scared, I guess, that I'm going to fail all of you . . . I mean . . . Sorry, I mean that I'm *having the thought* that I'm going to fail all of you and I am feeling nervous. I am . . . having the thought that I am weak, and that I am not brave enough to protect you all.'

Eribelle smiles. 'Notice that all of us struggle with similar thoughts of self-inadequacy. This brings me to the second step in our Moon Tradition practice – *Common Humanity.* Common Humanity is the realisation that you are not alone in your experience, and that others struggle with very similar thoughts and feelings as you do. For example, raise your hand if back at the consulate you considered putting on the choker to escape the effects of the Fusion Potion.'

You and the legion, except for Talia, each timidly raise a hand.

'But if everyone feels the same, then why do we feel so alone?' Lex asks as all of you put your hands down.

'Most of us feel so much shame about these experiences that we shut down and don't express or address them. The less we connect with these, the more we numb and disconnect, the more shame we feel.'

'Are you saying that people who numb their feelings suffer more?' Lex asks, visibly tearing up.

'Yes,' Eribelle answers, sorrow in her voice.

Lex looks over at Talia, who is still sitting and staring blankly, the choker around her neck blinking red. Your own heart aches for both of them. You look around and see Eribelle and the rest of the legion looking at Lex and Talia, their own hearts evidently hurting as well.

You have the bittersweet realisation that all of you are in this together. All of you are feeling these emotions together, fighting for something meaningful, even though it's hard, the hardest thing you've ever had to do. Why didn't you recognise that before? It seems obvious now. And for the first time in a long time, you feel a new emotion – hope.

Eribelle continues, 'The best way that we can help Talia and the best chance we have at defeating Mallena is to now practise the third element of the Moon Tradition – *Loving Kindness,* which means offering love and compassion for ourselves and others. Loving kindness is the most essential component of any white magic practice.

'You will need to pair up for this practice,' she continues. She points to you and Michael. 'Why don't the two of you pair up? Celeste, why don't you partner up with Java? Gherk and Anka. Lex and—'

'I'm with Talia,' Lex says in a stern voice.

'Lex,' Eribelle starts, sympathetically, 'the whole point of this is for you and your partner to help each other heal. If you partner with Talia, she won't—'

'I'm working with Talia,' says Lex, taking a seat on the floor opposite the stone-faced vampire.

'OK,' says Eribelle. To the rest of you, she says, 'Please sit facing your partner in the same way as Lex and Talia are sitting.'

Everyone follows her instructions. As you face Michael, Gherk removes a dozen pots and pans from his apron before getting comfortable on the floor facing Anka.

'Please take a few moments to really look at your partner's face,' Eribelle instructs. 'See their eyes, cheeks and mouth.'

You look at Michael's dark brown eyes. They look heavy and weary, and carry much sadness to them. You notice that he swallows when you make eye contact, his eyes momentarily filling up with tears. However, the tightening of his lips and the tightening of his face allow the tears to disappear again. In following Eribelle's instruction, you notice his dark brown nose, high cheekbones and tiny wrinkles around his lips. You imagine that these might have formed when he used to smile.

'As you're looking at your partner, take a moment to acknowledge that the being sitting in front of you was once a small child, just like you were. And was at one point or another extremely scared, happy or hopeful. This individual has experienced love, heartbreak and rejection, *just like you . . .*'

Looking at the giant soldier in front of you, you can now see him as a small child, someone who laughed and cried, someone who wanted to fit in, be accepted and valued. Just as you do. If only you could somehow protect that child and tell him that things will turn out OK.

Eribelle continues, 'Take a moment to realise that *just like you* the being in front of you wants to be loved and accepted, and wants to make a difference in the lives of others . . .'

You imagine little Michael being hurt and bullied by others. You imagine him being hurt and bullied by his own critical thoughts.

'. . . and now, if possible, please place your hands, paws or wings on your heart centre to activate your heart magic . . .'

You do as Eribelle instructs and feel the warmth radiate through your chest as the healing power of white magic builds inside you. As Michael puts his big hands on his own heart, you notice his body becoming calmer and more centred, before emitting a light silvery glow.

'. . . Now we are going to practise activating white magic to send healing from your heart to your partner's. We are going to use a Loving Kindness spell. Please repeat it while focusing on healing your partner . . .'

You look into Michael's eyes and he looks directly into yours. You swallow, recognising that just as you'd be sending healing wishes to Michael, he would be sending healing to you as well. For a moment, you feel naked and very vulnerable. But you continue.

Eribelle begins reciting the Loving Kindness spell. 'May you be happy . . .'

You repeat the phrase to Michael, feeling your own heart radiating warmth toward him. At the same time, you hear everyone else in the room repeat it out loud, before Eribelle continues. As she says each line, you all repeat it in turn.

'May you be free from pain and suffering . . .

'May you know how loved you are . . .

'May you know how much you matter . . .'

Tears roll down Michael's cheeks but his eyes are full of determination, focused on you and the words. You both sniffle at the same time. You're all healing as silvery light envelops the room.

'Now, please close your eyes for a moment and please keep connecting with your heart.'

You close your eyes, still feeling the warmth of your hands on your heart. It almost feels as if your heart is wrapped in a soft, warm and fuzzy blanket.

Eribelle continues, 'And now take a moment to consider that just like your partner, and just like everyone else in this room, you too deserve to be happy, and you too deserve to be loved and accepted . . .'

You take in a deep breath. Around you, you are hearing other deep breaths and some sniffling.

'. . . perhaps now remembering yourself as a small child, someone who at one point or another was extremely scared, happy or hopeful. A child who might have experienced love, heartbreak and rejection . . .'

Your eyes burn with tears as you are bombarded with images of yourself as a small child, the many times you felt that you didn't quite fit in, that you were somehow 'different', the many times you were teased for being 'too sensitive'.

As if reading your mind, Eribelle coaches you: '. . . and if you find yourself getting carried away by your memories, take a breath and gently focus on the sensation of your feet as they are making contact with the ground. Take a moment to remind yourself that at this very moment, your feet are right Here on the ground and you are safe.'

You take a breath and concentrate on feeling your feet, the weight of them, the pressure of the floor against them. You notice your anxiety beginning to subside, feeling yourself becoming more present in the present moment.

'And now bring your focus back to feeling the warmth of your heart, reminding yourself that just like the people around you, you too are worthy of love and acceptance. And with your eyes closed, please send yourself the Loving Kindness wishes . . .'

Again you feel almost naked and vulnerable, but you repeat the phrases after she says them, one by one, just as everyone else does.

'May I be happy . . .

'May I be free from pain and suffering . . .

'May I know how loved I am . . .

'May I know how much I matter . . .'

The sniffles around you are louder and you feel your own tears stinging your cheeks.

'Now please open your eyes and look at your partner . . .'

You open your eyes and look at Michael. He smiles at you, his face wet from tears. You smile back.

'. . . and with your eyes focused on your partner, please repeat these magical phrases to finalise the healing for you both . . .

'May we be happy . . .

'May we be free from pain and suffering . . .

'May we know how loved we are . . .

'May we know how much we matter.'

Your heart is lighter than you ever remember it feeling. You feel peace, joy and somehow bittersweet sorrow, all at the same time. Given the energy around you, you imagine that others feel the same way.

'Eribelle!' Lex shouts.

Everyone turns to face the elf, who is shaking. Talia's eyes are back to their usual vibrant red colour and tears are visible on her face.

Eribelle runs over to them and grabs Talia's hands. 'Talia! Talia, can you hear me?'

But the vampire doesn't seem to hear. You watch as the colour slowly fades again from Talia's eyes, returning to stone-cold grey.

'No!' Lex shouts, pushing Eribelle out of the way and grabbing Talia, shaking her. 'Talia! Talia, come back!'

Lex tugs at the choker but it won't budge. Eribelle places one of her hands on Lex's shoulder and the other on the elf's heart. The two stare at each other for a moment, Eribelle taking slow, deep breaths and looking into Lex's eyes. You see a bubble of light, silvery energy emanate from Eribelle and cloak itself around Lex, who seems calmer now.

'I think that whatever that was, was a good sign,' Eribelle says. 'I think there is still a chance that we might be able to save her but I don't exactly know how.'

'When, then?' Lex pleads. 'Whatever it takes, please do it.'

'I may know someone who might be able to help – a neuroscientist, who specialises in studying the effects of the Moon Tradition practice on the brain. He might know how to break the choker.'

'Great! Let's go! Let's go right now.'

'Just a moment,' Eribelle says.

She takes off her golden moon necklace with its crimson heart and places it around Talia's neck. The vampire's eyes redden again for a brief moment but then revert to grey.

Eribelle smiles. 'There is hope.'

'Thank you. Thank you so much,' Lex says.

Less than ten minutes later, you all make your way down the rope, Gherk carrying Talia.

It is still night. A beautiful moon illuminates the sky, silver and perfectly full. The others start walking, but you take a moment to yourself. Your back is stiff and sore from all the sitting and climbing. You stop to stretch and breathe in the crisp night air, and the tension starts to reduce. Satisfied, you walk briskly to catch up with the legion, but then stop. There's a rustling in the branches. You turn in the direction of the noise and a pair of large yellow eyes stares back at you from the bushes. A creature bursts forth, its enormous size a direct match for its massive teeth and claws. You've only previously seen such creatures in books and movies, but there is no mistake about it. It is, in fact, a werewolf.

You're stunned into silent terror, your heart pounding, unable to even think to call out for help. Your eyes are fixed on the nightmare in front of you. The creature puffs out its gigantic chest as it stands on its hind legs and howls. Then, as you turn to run and open your mouth to yell, the werewolf tackles you to the ground, knocking the wind from your lungs as its sharp teeth bare inches from your face.

It bites your shoulder and everything goes black . . .

Proceed to page 179.

'Uh, dinner is, uh, ready,' Gherk calls.

Anka assists you in standing and walking over to the picnic area that Gherk has set up.

'How are you feeling?' Blake asks you cautiously.

'Better, thanks,' you respond and then add, 'Look, about before . . .'

'Don't worry about it,' he says.

You sit next to Lex, who is looking pale and defeated. 'How is Talia?'

'The same,' Lex replies flatly. 'Blake was trying a few things but none of them are working.'

'What do you know so far?' you ask Blake.

'Well, from what we know from neuroscience research, emotional numbing like this is likely due to a significant reduction of certain essential chemicals, such as dopamine, serotonin and oxytocin. In most people, a reduction of these chemicals causes catatonic depression, where the person is so miserable that they might appear stupefied.'

'So if we find a way to increase these chemicals in Talia's body, will that break the choker?' you ask.

'I'm not sure,' he responds, 'but I think that at the very least it might give us more time to figure out how to break it.'

'When Lex was practising the Moon Tradition with Talia, there was a breakthrough,' you mention.

'Yes, Lex told me,' Blake says. 'It makes a lot of sense, since the Moon Tradition can stimulate the production of many of these chemicals, especially oxytocin. We tried to recreate it and were not successful. Talia would have moments where she would make eye contact with Lex, but would then become numb again. I think we are on the right track but we need to keep trying.'

'No offence, Blake,' says Michael, 'but how many of these chokers have you cracked in your life?'

'None,' Blake says, lowering his head.

Michael purses his lips. 'Then why are you giving Lex a false sense of hope?'

'Because hope is all we have right now,' says Blake.

You take a bite of a grey carrot. Just like the sweet in Borreus' hut, it tastes like chalk. It tastes like chalk and then like nothing at all. 'Umm, Gherk? Are these vegetables fresh? They taste a little . . . funny.'

'What? Oh no!' The ogre was so busy serving everyone else that he did not try the food himself.

He tries a piece of grey toast, then a tomato, then a piece of a grey roasted potato and a boring-grey piece of steak. His eyes grow wider and wider with each bite. He starts to tremble, sweat forming on his forehead. 'Oh, no, no, no!' He slumps to the ground, shaking.

'Gherk, listen to me,' Eribelle says, putting her tiny hands on his massive cheeks. 'You did not poison the food. The food is fine.'

'But . . . it's, uh . . .' His lower lip trembles. 'The food . . . is, uh, no good.'

Eribelle sighs. 'I'm guessing that you cannot see colours or you would see that all the food has turned grey. It isn't your cooking, Gherk. It's Mallena's magic. The numbing. The nothingness. It's spreading.'

'Talia!' Lex shouts and runs toward her.

Talia's image begins to flicker and fade.

'Talia! Talia! Please! No!' Lex is holding the vampire's face, then looks up at Blake. 'She feels so cold.'

Blake looks crestfallen. 'I am so sorry, Lex,' he says. 'That's how my sister went out too. I'm afraid there's nothing more we can do.

If there's any consolation, once she dies, there's a chance you won't remember her, though given your strong emotional connection to her, that's highly unlikely. I've certainly never forgotten my sister . . .'

'SHUT UP! JUST STOP TALKING!' Lex screams. 'I don't want to forget her! I love her! OK? I don't want—'

'What's that?' Michael asks, pointing up and behind Lex.

You turn. 'Katrina!'

Katrina is riding on Hektor's shoulders as he flies about ten feet above the ground, Hera flying closely behind them. Katrina jumps off the dragopurr and runs toward Lex and Talia.

'Lex! What happened? Are you OK?'

Lex shakes their head, arms tightly wrapped around the translucent vampire. You feel sick watching this, wishing you could do something, wishing you could save Talia or comfort Lex. You cannot watch it but you can't look away. You watch Talia's last disappearing moments as Hera approaches Lex and Talia, sniffing them. Suddenly, the young dragopurr leaps, tackling them both to the ground.

'Hera! Hera! What are you doing? Get off!' Katrina screams, trying to move the feline, but to no avail.

Hera hisses and growls at Katrina to keep away, covering both Talia and Lex with her enormous body.

Michael rushes over to help but Blake holds him back. 'Wait.'

'What?' Michael snaps. 'My friends are under that animal. We need to move it!'

'Wait,' Blake says again. 'I think it's trying to help.'

You hold your breath, standing back with everyone else, watching the scene in front of you. A few minutes later, Hera begins to purr and gently stands. You see Lex's arms still wrapped around Talia, who is looking solid now.

You rush over to them, as does everyone else. Lex is crying.

'Talia,' Lex cries, holding Talia's hands, the elf's voice breaking at times. 'Talia, can you hear me? Please. Please come back . . . Look, I want you to know that I understand why you did it. I know it hasn't been easy for you. I know you spend every day shaming yourself for the way that you look and for what he did to you. I know how hard that is. But it's not your fault. He was the perpetrator. You didn't do anything wrong . . . I know that your life hasn't been easy, but please know that if you choose to stay, you won't have to face it alone . . . Please know how loved you are. How incredibly beautiful you are. To me, you're perfect in every way . . . I love you, Talia . . .'

CRACK!

The choker splits open, pieces shattering on the ground. The centrepiece blinks red a few more times until it goes out for ever. Colour begins to settle back into the atmosphere and into everyone's hearts. Your heart and your eyes burn with joy.

'I heard you,' Talia finally says to Lex. 'I heard you back at the fairy-hut and I heard you just now . . . Thank you. Thank you for everything you said.'

Lex smiles at the same time as Talia wraps her arms around the tearful elf, and the two exchange a soft, passionate kiss.

You look away out of courtesy, but smile, feeling as if your heart is singing. You then turn to Blake. 'Will I always be able to feel this happy for others?'

'You mean, *empathic joy?*' he asks. 'Yes, the ability to be empathically happy for others does not go away with being a werewolf. At times it might be harder, especially if you yourself are struggling. Always remember that you are a human first and werewolf last. It isn't who you are; it is something that happened to you. How you respond to it is up to you.'

You nod in understanding. To your left you overhear Michael telling Katrina about surviving the Fusion Potion.

'I know exactly what I would fuse with,' Katrina says.

'What?' he asks.

'It would have been, "You're so ugly. No one will ever love you unless you lose weight." Something to that effect.'

'That's really sad,' Michael says.

'I know. Pathetic, really.'

'No,' he says. 'I mean that it is sad that you think that, because I think you are the most beautiful woman I have ever met.'

You sneak a peek in their direction, just in time to notice Katrina blushing as she lowers her gaze and then looks back up at him, tears sparkling in her large brown eyes. 'Thank you.' She sniffles. 'Oh, gosh, I'm such a mess.'

He smiles at her. 'Yes, you are.'

She laughs and fixes her hair. 'It's funny, I always thought you didn't like me.'

'What gave you that idea?' he says, sounding genuinely surprised.

'You were always so mean to me.'

'Oh. Yes. I was. I know I was . . . I'm sorry. I'm mean to everyone but it doesn't make it right. And it doesn't mean I don't like you.'

'Well, you're going to have to work on that, the being mean thing,' she says, half-smiling. 'It's not very nice.'

'Yes, ma'am,' he responds, smiling back.

You turn away from them to give them some privacy and find yourself smiling again. *Empathic joy. I kind of like it.*

'I think I figured it out,' Blake says, interrupting your moment.

Everyone turns to face him. Blake is holding pieces of the broken choker in his hands. 'I think I figured out how the choker works and how we were able to break it. The choker seems to shut down the three main components necessary for connection in mammals. These components are soothing speech, soft touch and physical warmth. Lex, you've been able to establish the first two with Talia by using the Moon Tradition and holding Talia's hands. I had not considered the importance of the third component until Hera was able to provide it for Talia. Physical warmth – such as that we receive from a warm blanket, or from snuggling with a cat or, in this case, being cuddled by a dragopurr. I think that taken together, these three components filled Talia's body with the very chemicals that the choker was blocking when it was causing Talia to experience excruciating depression. If I am correct, then we might have the formula for destroying the other chokers.'

'Does that include Mallena's?' you ask.

'We can't be sure,' Michael says. 'She does not seem to be experiencing depression, at least not when I last saw her. Either she is not affected by the choker the same way, or her magic can somehow withstand its negative effects.'

'The other issue with Mallena is that her magic is far superior to what I can support or block,' Celeste says.

'Me too,' Eribelle agrees. 'I've actually been thinking about this. Can we somehow block her from being able to expel magic from her hands?'

'Want me to chop them off?' Michael asks.

'No!' Anka responds quickly. 'Ve vill not fight violence viz violence.'

'How then?' Michael asks.

'Hmm,' Blake ponders, rubbing his chin. 'I wonder . . .' He puts his hands into the pockets of his pink suit and takes out a pink glove from each pocket.

'We are going to dress her up?' Michael sneers.

'Michael!' Katrina gives him a stern look.

'Sorry,' he says. 'Please continue.'

'Mallena's power, as with most magic, is an extension of her body energy, focused by her physical movement and projected from her fingertips. If we were to somehow numb her fingers, maybe she wouldn't be able to use her magic.'

'Kind of like jamming a gun?' Michael asks.

'Precisely,' Blake says. 'We need to figure out a way to numb her hands, somehow, to block her magic. Celeste, do you think there is a way?'

'*Hielo!*' Celeste says. 'Ice spell. I can charm the gloves so that when anyone wears them, their hands will turn to ice.'

'Perfect! The freezing should stop her nerve endings from firing, so hopefully she won't be able to use her magic.'

'All right then,' Michael says. 'That's all settled. Let's get ready to go.'

'I hate to say this,' Blake says, 'but I think that we should wait out the night and go in the morning.'

'Are you kidding?' Michael says as the vein in his left temple visibly pulsates so much that it looks like it is going to pop. 'We have less than forty-eight hours left and you want to sleep Here?'

'Blake is right,' Anka says. 'Mallena's traps are dangerous even in the daylight. If ve go at night, ve are sure to fail. Ve vill go in ze morning.'

Everyone looks at you.

If you choose to go to Mallena's castle immediately, go to page 109.

If you choose to wait until morning, go to page 126.

Avoidance

Lose 3 wisdom points

As disgusting as the sight is, avoiding looking at it will only make you feel more repulsed. If you don't believe me, try it. Try to first visualise that revolting scene – the cockroaches, the ants, the filthy table. Really picture all the details.

Got it? Good.

Now, close your eyes for one minute and do everything you can to erase this image from your mind. Do NOT think of the filthy table, or even the words 'filthy', 'table', 'cockroaches' or 'ants'.

Ready? Go!

. . .

How did that go? Most people find that they are unable to completely stop thinking about these images. Just when we try to focus on something else, there's an image of a creepy cockroach with its grotesque antennas peeking out from behind your mind.

Now, let's try the opposite.

Close your eyes and do everything you can to focus on the image of the disgusting table with all the insects. Focus on the roaches and ants. Don't take your focus off them for the entire minute. Just watch them as closely as possible.

Go!

. . .

What did you notice? Chances are you got distracted or bored after some time and were no longer thinking of the table. In the future, rather than avoiding upsetting thoughts and images, try to concentrate on them and study them. It seems to be a much better approach.

Continue to page 6.

Impulsivity

Lose 10 wisdom points

Sometimes we might rush to make a decision without carefully weighing out all the choices. Acting on an impulse is likely to make it more difficult for you to reach your goals, as opposed to taking your time to make careful steps toward your mission.

This same consideration applies to other life situations. For instance, it might not make sense to run for five kilometres for someone who is just starting to exercise. In fact, doing so would likely set them back as they might injure themselves and might not be able to exercise for a long time after that.

In this case, you get caught by the Minotaurs at Mallena's castle, who bring you back to the consulate. Java and the dragopurrs get shot and killed in the process. Time runs out. Mallena wins.

The end.

GO BACK TO THE BEGINNING AND TRY AGAIN.

Celeste gently cradles and caresses the raven's black feathers. Java looks so stiff now that he reminds you of a Halloween decoration rather than a living creature. Once so impressive, so large and animated, now small, helpless and still. Celeste presses him to her chest, some of her tears landing on Java's lifeless form.

Your heart feels like it has also been punctured with arrows. Your mind runs through several dozen scenarios, things you can try to say or do, but none of them seem to be enough. You look to Anka for guidance. She takes a few steps toward you and places her hand on your shoulder.

'Take ze pressure off yourself to fix it,' she says. 'If you vant to help her, zen just be Here viz her.'

You feel the tight bands around your heart beginning to loosen, feeling as if you can breathe again.

'Thanks,' you say to Anka and walk up to Celeste.

Eribelle and Blake are kneeling next to her. You kneel on the ground opposite her.

'Celeste, I am so sorry,' you say. 'I wish there were something I could do.'

You feel both helpless and stupid, but to your surprise, Celeste lifts her head and gives you a small smile through the tears.

'Thanks,' she says, sniffling, inhaling her own pain.

You sit in the circle, which slowly expands as the rest of the legion members stagger to join in. You place your own hands on your heart, breathing with her, in a circle of grief and compassion.

After some time, Eribelle moves the earth beneath her, creating a small hole. She and Celeste then pull purple magic together to entwine branches, leaves and flowers, weaving a small coffin. Celeste gently lowers Java into the coffin, breathing heavily, not blinking. She emits golden and purple light from her hands as she lowers the floral casket into the hole in the ground. Satisfied, she takes a breath and buries the coffin with her bare hands. First slowly and gently. Then faster and faster, almost maniacally, in a state of panic, her breathing becoming faster and shallower, until she collapses on the ground above it and sobs.

You stand there, watching, mourning alongside the others. Lex and Talia hold one another as they both cry. Gherk blows his nose loudly on a banquet tablecloth he is using as a handkerchief. Even the dragopurrs have stopped their usual shenanigans and are cuddling up with Katrina. You realise how much you are noticing your emotions at this time. It is both devastating and strangely soothing to witness so much grief around you and how the group is grieving together. Maybe oxytocin, that magical chemical Blake and Eribelle mentioned earlier, is also released in times of grief.

Finally, Celeste stands. 'Thank you so much, everyone,' she says. 'Thank you for all your support. It means so much to me. I know it means a lot to Java too.' She chokes back a sob as she continues. 'I . . . I didn't . . . I didn't support him enough . . .'

'Celeste, don't—' Lex starts.

'No, Lex, it's true,' Celeste argues. 'I frequently told him that his jokes weren't funny and that he needed to be more serious, or to pay more attention. But the truth is . . . the truth is that he was the funniest bloody bird I've ever met.' She cries while smiling at the same time. 'You know, he used to be such a prankster too. There was one time that my nursing programme supervisor, Jake, was being rude to me and Java made a loudspeaker announcement, wishing Jake a very happy birthday.' She laughs at the memory. 'It wasn't Jake's birthday, of course, but Java led the entire hospital in singing "Happy Birthday" to Jake . . . He did always want to become a comedian . . .'

'I guess the joke is on him now,' Abbott remarks, startling you. You've been so preoccupied by the funeral, you'd completely forgotten the Minotaur tied to a tall redwood. You hadn't even realised it was Abbott until now.

'Watch it!' Blake snarls at him.

'Or what?' the agent snaps back, his crooked mouth shaking as he sniggers. 'You and your ugly friends are gonna beat me up? Please! Go back to where you came from, Lyke, and take the fugly ogre with you.'

Blake growls as his face extends and his arms stretch out. 'No!' he shouts to himself, stopping the metamorphosis and returning to his human shape.

'Couldn't do it, eh?' Abbott smirks. 'Pathetic. You—'

A punch in the face from Michael silences the obnoxious Minotaur. He droops forward, his body supported by Celeste's ropes.

'Thanks,' says Blake. 'Not sure how much I would have been able to hold out.'

'No problem,' Michael responds. He turns to Hoffman, still tangled in one of Eribelle's nets. 'What about you, Dayton? Do you have something to say?'

'Nothing,' Hoffman answers, narrowing his eyebrows.

As Michael and Hoffman stare each other down, you walk over to Blake and ask, 'How did you stop mid-transformation?'

'Most people think that lycanthropy is all-or-nothing, that either you're a werewolf or you're not. But in reality, while we don't always have a choice about what happens to us, we always have a choice how we respond to events and changes.'

'What do you mean?' you ask, intrigued.

'My mum used to say that we all have two wolves inside us – the dark and the light. The dark one is violent, impulsive and mean. The light one is thoughtful, careful and caring. The wolf that survives is the one that you feed.'

'Intense,' you say, pondering his words. 'Was your mum a werewolf too?'

'No,' he says. 'But my dad was. Guess which wolf he fed? I'll give you a hint. It wasn't the light one. He killed her one evening when they were arguing.'

'Oh, Blake. I'm sorry.'

'Want to know what they were arguing about? Pizza toppings. She forgot the anchovies, apparently, and he morphed right in front of me and bit her head off. Literally. Funny that he always thought I'd be grateful to him for making me what I am. I never wanted this. I am so sorry to have inflicted this upon you too.'

'But you manage? You cope?'

'I try. Some days are worse than others.'

'And what was that thing that Abbott called you? A Lyke?'

'It's a slur. About the worst thing you can call my kind. Well . . . our kind.'

At that moment, Beethoven's *Moonlight Sonata* plays.

'What the bloody hell is that?' Michael asks.

'My mobile phone,' Hoffman responds. His usually calm speech is pressured now. 'It's my wife. I have to answer it.'

'Not a chance,' Michael scoffs.

Hoffman looks directly at you. His eyes connect with yours and you see his pain, his dried-up tears, the years of suffering and desperation. 'She has cancer. She's dying. She might need something. Please.'

'Don't even think about it,' Michael says to you.

'You can put it on speaker if you'd like. Please. Just let me talk to her.'

'Let him answer it,' you say, and you walk up to Michael.

Michael pulls the phone out of Hoffman's jacket. You can read the caller ID: Carmen Hoffman, with a small red heart displayed after it.

'I'm warning you, Dayton, not one word out of place,' Michael says, pressing the speakerphone button.

'Oh, uh, hello?' greets a female voice on the other end of the phone. She sounds weak and exhausted.

'Yes, hello, sweetheart,' Hoffman's voice is soft and reassuring. 'Is everything all right?'

'Dayton, honey, when are you coming home?'

'Soon, honey. Very soon.'

'You said that two weeks ago.' She sounds so sad.

'I know, honey. I'm sorry,' Hoffman says, lowering his head and shaking it side to side.

'Look, whatever Mallena promised you, it isn't worth it. Please, just come home.'

His voice sounds firmer now when he responds, 'I can't. Not yet.'

There is a sound of sniffling and then: 'Please, Dayton. I'm scared. I just want you Here with me.'

'I will be with you as soon as I can, my love. Please, just trust me.'

'Always. I always trust you. I love you, Dayton.'

'I love you too, sweetheart,' Hoffman says, his breath getting heavier.

Carmen hangs up. Hoffman is quiet for a few moments before turning to you and Michael. 'Thanks.'

Michael doesn't respond, only puts Hoffman's phone back in his jacket.

'It's nearly morning,' Lex notes. 'We need to go.'

'I hope you know the ramifications of what you're about to do,' Hoffman warns.

'You're not the only one who used to work with her, Dayton,' Michael snaps. 'Some of us aren't afraid to stand up to her.'

'She will use what you love the most to make you more afraid than you have ever been in your life.'

'That's what happened to you,' you realise. Hoffman lowers his head as you continue. 'It's your wife. Mallena is using your wife as leverage.'

Hoffman doesn't say anything.

'You can walk away,' you say. 'Whatever she's threatening you with isn't worth this.'

'I can't. I just can't,' Hoffman says.

'We need to get going,' Michael says.

After ten minutes of preparation, you're all ready to continue. Mallena's castle is roughly four hours east on foot.

'If we fly—' Michael suggests before Katrina quickly starts shaking her head.

'I'm not flying,' she says.

'But you flew here.'

'Sure. We were flying just a few feet off the ground. If we can maintain that height, that would be fine.'

'Katrina,' Blake says, 'it would take a lot longer to fly that low. We need to, at the very least, stay above the trees.'

'If you want to fly that high, you'll have to go without me.'

'Katrina,' Michael says, taking her hand, 'the dragopurrs only listen to you. We can't go without them and they won't go anywhere without you. I know that you are afraid but—'

'Either we fly low or we are not flying,' Katrina says sternly, pulling her hand away.

'Well, you heard the lady,' Michael sighs. 'I guess we are flying low.'

Katrina holds out two pieces of salmon for the felines, who lick them off her hands. She secures the harness on them and helps the others load up the supplies on top of the furry beasts. Everyone still seems sombre and subdued. Even the dragopurrs aren't as playful as they normally are.

Gherk, Katrina, Anka, Lex and Talia climb on top of Hektor, and the rest of you fly on Hera. The felines take off with a run on Katrina's command. They dash along the forest floor, avoiding the trees until they reach a clearing where the trees are more spread out and open.

'Up!' Katrina yells, and the dragopurrs push off the ground and leap into the air. They remain no higher than ten feet off the ground, though their speed allows you to travel nearly five times faster than you would have at a full-speed run.

The gentle sound of the feline wings is somehow soothing to your ears. The morning breeze on your face feels wonderful and you notice the tops of purple, yellow and scarlet flowers underneath you. Up ahead you see the eerie outline of the castle. There is a wooden drawbridge leading up to it over an expansive moat. The moat water looks eerily still and dark. The sun burns into the stark limestone walls, reflecting the impenetrability of the castle while cloaking its many battlements. The murder holes and machicolations hide in the shadows.

As you get closer, there's a familiar grey filter – the flowers no longer look colourful, the sun in the sky looks rather like a dimming light bulb, and the clouds look dead and gloomy. You wonder if this will be the last time you see daylight of any kind. Your stomach churns and you exhale, realising that you've been holding your breath. You look down and see your reflection in the darkness of the murky water.

What is that?

You hold back a scream, so as not to scare the others, but there's no mistake about it: the figure looking back at you is your own skeleton. It moves as you do, but it has no skin and no clothing. You swallow, trying not to think about what this might mean.

I am Here, my feet are Here, and right now I am safe.

WHOOSH!

The dragopurrs hit something hard, something invisible. They meow and hiss in all directions, but are unable to move. There's a jerking sensation as your body is yanked several feet up. You and the others are squished together.

'What's happening?' you ask.

'I believe ve are caught in a net,' Anka says. 'Invisible net or rope.'

Indeed, Hektor and Hera, as well as their passengers, are being thrashed around as the invisible trap elevates. The dragopurrs continue meowing as they claw at the walls of their captivity. Finally, Hera's patience runs out. She hisses and arches her body, nearly throwing you off. She stops for a moment, takes in a deep breath, then exhales a large, wide jet of flame directly in front of her. Hektor follows suit.

The fire seems to be sucked out through some kind of a netted pattern, confirming that you are, in fact, in a giant, invisible net. However, the net itself does not seem to have suffered any damage from the fire breathers. Your skin begins to burn from the heat around you but the felines are not giving up.

'Stop!' Katrina shouts at them but the felines do not seem to be paying attention. Visibly freaked out by being restricted, the dragopurrs are flailing, hissing, meowing and spitting fire. You and the others are barely hanging on, and are trying not to get singed. Katrina is nearly hoarse from screaming at the giant cats, who are still not listening to anything she says.

The net begins to rock from side to side, barely noticeable at first, and then the motion is more and more ferocious. The felines stop meowing, their green eyes as wide as everyone else's.

'Aaaaah!' most of you shout as the net drops sharply, your stomach feeling as if you are in a rapidly falling aeroplane.

The net slows down but is still lowering, the morbid death water inching closer.

'We can't go into that water!' Michael yells.

'What will it do?' Lex asks.

'I don't know. But whatever it is, it's not going to be good.'

'Katrina! Can you make the dragopurrs fly higher?' Michael asks.

'How much higher?' she asks with trepidation in her voice.

'Away from the water!'

'Hektor! Hera! Up! *Up! UP!*' she shouts at the felines.

The dragopurrs attempt to open their wings but are restricted by an invisible force. Hektor meows in pain, as Hera hisses, and they both lower their wings.

'They can't!' Katrina screams, with panic in her voice. 'What do we do?'

'Let me try something,' Celeste calls. After taking a large and quick swig of her coffee, she closes her eyes in concentration.

'Any time now!' Michael shouts.

'Give me a minute!' she snaps, her eyes still closed, moving her hands palm down and pushing the air away. Purple and golden sparks fly out of her hands. The net jerks but is still lowering.

Eribelle throws several pinches of fairy dust at the net but it does nothing.

All of you watch in horror as the meowing, screaming dragopurrs approach the daunting water. Their paws are first to touch the surface, which mists and sizzles. Hera pulls away one paw, then another, trying to keep out of the water. Hektor is frozen with fear.

117

You lift your legs closer to you to delay the inevitable as the dragopurrs descend deeper under water. Realising you're holding your breath, you force yourself to let it out, then take in another breath as you place your hands on your heart and prepare for excruciating pain.

But it doesn't come. Instead of excruciating impact, your legs experience a light, cool mist, soothing and eerie at the same time.

No one moves now. No one says a word.

The dragopurrs land at the bottom of the misty lake. The water seems to be above you and schools of fish of various colours – orange, blue and green – swim meditatively by you. They are exuding light, similar to fireflies. It is mesmerising. Even with the water above you, you're able to breathe and, in fact, are breathing steadily. It's odd but standing in this beautiful environment, feeling the cool, soothing moisture in the air, it's suddenly very calming compared to so many of your recent experiences. You don't remember the last time you felt this serene.

The dragopurrs are calm and peaceful now too, having settled on the ground, purring. You and the rest of the legion hop off them, and take the opportunity to lounge and recover. For some reason, this scenery reminds you of a book you read a long time ago. You don't remember what it was called. Just that it read like a dream.

The ogre is smiling at you with a happy, dazed look on his face. *What's his name again?*

The fairy stretches out her wings next to you and reaches for the nearby seaweed. She grabs a few stems and folds them together, wearing it as a wreath as she hums to herself. To your right, the witch picks up a small twig and begins to draw in the sand. You watch her thoughtful, hypnotic strokes with peaceful curiosity. She draws a circle, then evolves it into a more distinct shape with a hooked nose, some feathers and wings. The bird looks familiar somehow.

'Is this your bird?' you ask her.

'My raven, yes.' She smiles. 'Isn't he lovely?'

'What is his name?' you ask.

'Java,' she says, still smiling as tears trickle down her face.

'Why are you crying?'

'I . . . I don't know. I miss him, I guess.'

You smile at her in understanding. 'Well, I hope you will see him soon enough.'

'Thanks. I hope so too.'

'Gah!' the Ukrainian woman screams, grabbing her chest. As she does, you feel your own heart hurting.

'What's wrong? What is it?' the fairy asks her.

'Ve are dying here!'

'What?' you ask, surprised. 'What are you talking about?'

'Zis place! It is dangerous!'

'What do you mean?' you demand. 'This . . . I don't actually know what this place is but it's nice. I don't actually remember the last time I ever felt so nice.'

'Vhat do you remember?' she demands, grabbing you by your shoulders. 'Do you remember vhy ve came here?'

'No,' you admit, shaking your head as panic, familiar panic, spreads through you.

The others are now alarmed and confused. The witch still sniffles.

'Do any of you remember vhy ve are here?' she asks all of you.

Everyone shakes their head. You're getting frustrated and annoyed.

'Look . . . what is your name?'

'Anka.'

'Anka. Good. Look, why does it matter why we are here? We are safe. We feel good. Can't we just enjoy it?'

Anka's face becomes grey and ashen. She points to the witch. 'You are grieving.'

'What? What do you mean?' the witch asks. 'Grieving over whom?'

'I sink you know who.'

The witch looks around, confused. Then she looks down to her drawing. 'What? No! Java? No!' Her face becomes pale. She is trembling. She shakes her head from side to side and falls on top of the sand drawing, as if trying to cradle the picture. She sobs as she repeats the name, 'Java!'

'Ve have to remember vhy ve came Here or ve vill die Here.'

'How?' a tall, black, muscled man says. He looks like he could be a soldier. 'How do we remember?'

Anka grabs her chest. You can almost feel it in yours – a sharp, squeezing, penetrating pain.

'What's wrong?' the fairy asks her. 'Are you ill?'

'Yes,' Anka says, 'but zat is not vhat is important now. Ve are all dying.'

There is an eerie silence among all of you as Anka closes her eyes.

'I see it. Ze only hope ve have of getting out of Here is to connect viz vhat ve care about ze most, our *core values*.'

'How do we do that?' you ask.

'Ve have to realise zat ve are dying. And ve have to imagine zat ve lived our lives exactly as ve vant, in ze vay zat is most consistent viz our hearts. And zen . . .' She opens her eyes and sighs.

'And then what?' the elf asks.

'And zen ve have to write our own eulogy.'

'*What?*' several of you say at once.

'That's crazy!' the vampire shouts.

'Nope. Not doing it,' the soldier declares.

'Ve need to connect viz our core values. Ze best vay to identify zem is to see how ve vould like to live our lives.'

'And if we don't do it?' you ask, unsure if you want to hear the answer.

'If ve don't do it, ve vill forget to live.'

If you are willing to identify your core values and write out your eulogy, go to page 124.

If you are not willing to identify your core values, go to page 127.

Your head is pounding, the depression and shame in your stomach feeling like a bottomless pit of hell. Your eyes are burning with tears that won't come and your chest feels as if your heart was ripped out of it with sharp talons.

Mallena is still talking but it is nearly impossible to make out what she is saying, the tormenting voice of the Fusion Potion overshadowing all other senses.

'You are a failure. You are a coward. You can't handle this.'

Stop. Please. Stop, you try to plead with the voice in your mind. But it won't.

'PUT IT ON! You need to put on the choker or you will lose your mind. You will go crazy. You are going to lose control. You are going to pass out. And die. PUT IT ON!'

If you choose to avoid these painful thoughts and sensations by putting on the Painless Choker, go to page 75.

If you choose to ride out the Fusion Potion instead of escaping it, proceed to page 79.

Empathic Distress Toxin

Lose 3 inner strength points

Seeing other people struggling can cause our own levels of distress to increase as well. Feeling the emotions of other people is called *empathy,* an emotion most humans are able to feel, though some feel it more strongly than others. In fact, our brain is wired for empathy. We have special brain cells, called *mirror neurons,* which act the same way when we are in physical or emotional pain, or when we see others experiencing these.

Therefore, it is not surprising that witnessing other people's struggles can make us feel upset. This is called *empathic distress.* Empathic distress can make us feel less connected to others; it can make us feel physically and emotionally exhausted, as well as helpless and overwhelmed. When we experience empathic distress, we are less likely to help other people and ourselves.

To learn about how to reduce empathic distress, go to page 53.

Core Values

Gain 5 inner strength points

Core values allow us to have a direction in life. Core values can be thought of as different categories of things that are important to us, such as: family, friends, career, education, health, volunteering, creativity, spirituality, hobbies or pets. In addition, core values can include certain character strengths, such as: honour, compassion and integrity. Core values are different from goals in that goals are finite, whereas core values are life-long directions. For example, a goal might be to meet up with your friend for coffee, while a core value is to maintain your friendships.

Your core values might include standing up to injustice and tyranny and fighting to better the world in any way you are capable. Your value-driven actions might mean protecting those who are discriminated against, those who are being mistreated or misrepresented.

Many people live their lives without considering their core values and at the end of their lives, when they are on their death bed, people often regret not having followed their core values in the way that they would have liked. Most people's regrets are that they spent too much time working, not enough time with their friends and family, not enough time being themselves, and that they did not enjoy their life enough.

This exercise is meant to have you imagine that you are, in fact, at the end of your life, and to imagine that you've lived your life exactly as you would have wanted to, without any regrets. Perhaps it means that you made a difference in the lives of other people, or that you travelled the world, or enjoyed certain hobbies. From this exercise, you might be able to draw out ways that you can make changes to your life (if needed) in order to make your life more meaningful and desirable in the long run.

Please take some time now to write out your imagined eulogy, which could be said by someone who knew you really well. This person saw that you lived your life exactly how you wanted to, to the fullest. What would they say?

When you are finished, take some time to identify the specific categories that seem important to you, such as family, friends, education or others, and circle the ones you'd like to spend more time on. For example, if you value friendships but hardly make time to see your friends, circle that value and see if you can come up with some short-term goals to spend more time with your friends.

When you are finished with this task, please proceed to page 150.

Committed Action

Gain 5 wisdom points

Usually, the best way you can honour your commitments is to act in ways that are consistent with your core values – what you care about the most. Sometimes it makes the most sense to perform a small action, sometimes it makes the most sense to wait to perform an action, and sometimes a large action is needed. In most situations, acting out of impulse is more likely to set you back than to act with consideration for the outcomes. Given the danger of Mallena's powers, it makes the most sense to take your time and carefully evaluate your plan, as well as to travel to the castle when you have the best chance of succeeding – during daylight.

Proceed cautiously to page 172.

Lack of Core Values

Lose 5 inner strength points

Lack of identified core values can lead to us living out our lives in regret. Many people live out their lives buried in their work, forgetting what they're doing it for, forgetting the big picture, forgetting the things most important to them.

At the end of their lives, many people come to have regrets about having worked too hard, not spending enough time with the people they love or doing the things they care about.

If you would like to learn about how to identify your core values, turn back to page 124 but do not gain any points.

By the time you arrive at the Black Lake, the sun has already set. The moon is out in full view, so large and seeming so close that it looks like you could reach it, if you only had a tall ladder. Looking down, you realise how well Black Lake lives up to its name. It looks like it is made of precious onyx, its ebony waves magically twinkling in the moonlight. The waves crash against the boulders even though there is no wind.

'This is it,' Michael says. 'Serena's lake.'

'Where is she?' you ask.

Michael turns to face the rest of the legion. 'We all have to be fully mindful for her to arrive. Everyone, please, take three slow breaths and focus on your MESS marks.'

You all do as he instructs. There is a settling stillness with each breath and you take in the silence of the night. There is something tranquil about breathing together with your legion. As your own breath settles, the waves begin to settle too, and soon the lake is perfectly still, as is the legion.

A few moments later, there's a splash of water. You look up as a mermaid's head appears from the dark water. Her green hair shines in the moonlight, matching bits of seaweed that drape her. She smiles at all of you and gracefully pulls herself up on to a rock on the shore. She hasn't even spoken yet, but her majesty is astounding.

'Hello, Michael,' she says, her voice flowing like a warm summer breeze. 'How lovely it is to see you again.'

'You as well, Serena,' he says with a nod, before introducing you all.

'How can I be most helpful?' she asks.

'We were hoping you could tell us what happened between you and Mallena.'

'I can indeed. But I sense that there is much darkness in your voice. What makes you ask?'

'People are disappearing. Others are losing their memories or losing themselves.'

'Do you believe that it is connected to Mallena?'

'This might be a stretch but it started after you two stopped speaking,' Michael explains. 'She changed after that. She became controlling toward everything and everyone, harshly punishing anyone who disagreed with her. She's even trying to control everyone's emotions. I don't know why. None of us do. But this world is dying and we are desperate for information. Please.'

Serena sighs and considers this before speaking to the group. 'As Michael knows, Mallena and I used to meditate every week.'

Michael nods as Serena continues. 'We would meditate on sending love and healing to the beings of the universe. We practised in the Moon Tradition.'

'The Moon Tradition?' you ask.

'The Moon Tradition is the practice of sending love from your heart to the hearts of other beings. Mallena used to love this practice. She beamed with love and compassion for humanity. That is until her heart was broken.'

'Who broke her heart?' Talia asks.

'Humans. Mallena is, or rather *was*, an empath. She used to feel everyone's emotions as if they were her own,' Serena explains as she holds her heart with both of her hands. 'She used to cry over the hurt of others. She suffered when others did, her heart cracking with each human loss, until she could not take it any more. Her heart was so full of sorrow that it broke. The pain was so great, she said that she did not want to experience emotion ever again.'

'So that was when she stopped coming to see you?' Michael asks.

'Yes. I tried reaching out to her. I wrote her many letters but my ravens returned with them unopened. I have even tried contacting her heart with mine but her heart is not open to receive love from me or anyone else.'

'But, uh, is it not, uh, *safer* to have, uh, your heart closed? Is it not, uh, strength to not, uh, feel emotions?' Gherk asks.

Serena smiles sympathetically at him. 'You think as many humans do. In reality, to experience our emotions is both the scariest and also the most courageous thing anyone can do. What seems to be your biggest weakness is actually your biggest strength. Your raw emotions make you exceptional. They are what make you wonderful. Unfortunately, Mallena never fully understood this.'

'Is there anything else you could tell us that would help us stop her from destroying this world?' Michael asks.

'If my raven sources are correct, then she recently visited Borreus.'

'Borreus? The warlock from Soaring Mountain?' Celeste asks.

'The very same. I believe that she is searching for a spell to numb painful emotions.'

'How would a spell like that work, exactly?' Celeste asks.

'That I do not know,' Serena says. 'But I do hope that you are able to get more information. If anyone can help, it will be Borreus.'

'Right,' says Michael. 'We should stay here for the night. I'd hate to run into those hags at night.'

You all try to find the most comfortable place to sleep. You lie down on the grass under an old oak tree. You dream that you are back in school and you have to give a presentation in your history class. Only you did not prepare. Not even a little bit. As you open your mouth and try to speak, nothing comes out. Your teacher looks disappointed and then her face begins to melt. She is now a Faceless, grabbing you by the arm, shouting, 'You are a fraud!'

131

You awake with a gasp. It is sunrise, though you can still see the waxing gibbous moon. Serena has gone and you look around to try to find the legion. To your left, you see the dragopurrs cuddled up into a heart shape, their gigantic paws wrapped around one another. Katrina rests her head on Hektor's side as she sleeps.

To your right, you notice Talia checking out her own reflection in the water. She looks at herself sideways, gently resting her hands over her stomach. She then sucks in her gut and turns to look at herself from the other side. Her eyes narrow as her face shows grim disgust. Suddenly, she scrunches her face and punches herself in the stomach with both fists.

There's a familiar sense of shame in your stomach as you recall the many times you've also felt shame about your own appearance.

You run over to her. 'Talia! Talia! Stop!' You hold her fists away from her stomach until she stops fighting you. 'What are you doing?'

Her bottom lip trembles as tears run down her face. 'I . . . I . . . had . . . four vials,' she manages to get out between the sobs.

'What?'

'I . . . I try not to eat at all. As much as I can. But sometimes I'm so hungry that I can't stop myself. Sometimes I have two or three vials. When I'm stressed or tired, I have more.'

'Talia, everyone needs to eat. Everyone gets hungry.'

'You don't understand,' she sniffles. 'I *hate* hunger. It . . . I'm just so disgusted with myself,' she sobs again.

'I know I can't fix you,' you say. 'I know we're not going to solve this all right now. But I'm here if you need help. And . . . I hope one day you will come to know how beautiful you are, inside and out.'

You hold her for a while. You feel her body tension gradually settle.

'Thanks.' She finally smiles.

Once she seems to have relaxed, you walk over to check on the others. Katrina is currently using the clicker and salmon to reinforce the dragopurrs approaching the harness. The felines appear torn – on the one hand they want the salmon, but on the other hand, they do not like the harness. With some reluctance, they eventually give in to wearing the novel raiment in exchange for the treat.

You take a mindful moment to observe the world around you. Despite the apparent and impending doom, you notice that you are somehow more present and calmer than you have been in a long time. It is almost as if the upcoming end of the world made you more aware of the importance of the 'Here and Now'. You smile.

From overhead come the soft sounds of morning doves and blue finches, as well as other birds you cannot identify. Then you also hear gentle guitar strings. You walk toward it and find Lex strumming an acoustic model.

'You play?' you ask.

'No!' Lex jumps suddenly, the guitar remaining on the ground.

'It's OK, Lex,' you say, trying to sound reassuring. 'Don't listen to those hags. Their job was to make you doubt yourself.'

Lex sighs. 'You're right. It's just hard, you know? It's like they're in your head.'

'They kind of are. I think they feed on our mindless thoughts and magnify them. I think that's why when we were using the mindfulness spell, they disappeared.'

'I think you're right. It's certainly not easy to practise.'

'No,' you say, remembering your struggle with the Strah. 'It's not. Where did your guitar come from, anyway? I don't remember you carrying it.'

'Oh, I borrowed some of Celeste's potions.' Lex takes out a blue and a red vial from a jacket pocket. 'A few drops of the blue one and it shrinks, a couple of drops of the red one and it's back to full size.'

'Neat,' you say.

Not too far away from you, you hear Anka trying to help Gherk reduce his washing by practising mindfulness.

'At zis moment, right now, everysing is OK,' Anka reminds him. 'Notice ze feeling of ze vater on your hands as you vash zem . . . Very slowly . . . Good . . . Make sure zat you breeze . . . Breeze in . . . and breeze out.'

Gherk slows down his hand-washing and is visibly less distressed – his shoulders seem less tense and his body seems to have settled down. He is able to wash his hands for twenty minutes instead of his usual thirty.

'Good job, Gherk,' Anka says to him.

'Uh, thank you,' he says. And, for the first time since you've met him, he smiles.

After another hour, everyone is ready to travel once more. You head south toward Soaring Mountain. As you walk, you encounter several hags along the way. Some of them slither from behind trees and others are openly sitting on tree stumps.

'You are going to fail,' one of them hisses from behind a pine tree as it grabs your arm.

Your heart pounds as you begin to panic again.

'Vhere are your feet?' Anka asks you.

'My feet are Here,' you say, making sure to note the feeling of your feet and your heartbeat.

'Remind yourself zat ze hags might be scary but zey can't hurt you. Remind yourself zat you are Here and zat you are safe.'

You take a breath. 'I am Here. My feet are on the ground. And I am safe.'

After a few moments, the hag attacking you vanishes. Meanwhile, Anka assists the others with the mindfulness spell.

'I am, uh, Here. My, uh, feet are on the, uh, ground. And, uh, I am, uh, safe,' Gherk says to the two hags trying to pull him into anxiety.

The hags hiss and disappear. As you continue the journey, fewer show up and then finally they stop appearing altogether. You sigh with relief when you see the tall mountain in the distance.

Several uneventful hours later, you reach the base of a tall mountain. It is massive and its peak disappears somewhere in the clouds.

'Where exactly do we need to go?' you ask.

'Let's find out,' Celeste says after a large swig of her coffee. 'Java, can you please find out where on the mountain the warlock's house is? And maybe the best way to climb?'

'Just follow the golden brick road,' the raven replies jovially.

'Java!' Celeste snaps at him.

'I know, I know. No time for jokes . . . No time except the present time.' He flaps his wings and flies away before the witch gets a chance to curse him.

'I swear, teaching him to talk was probably one of the stupidest ideas I have ever had,' she mutters as she turns to Katrina. 'Do you think the dragopurrs can fly us up there?'

Katrina shakes her head. 'They are starting to approach the harness, which is a great sign, but they still won't let me put it on them. Not to mention that they have never flown with people. Testing it out while carrying us up a rocky mountain would not be safe.'

Michael gruffly remarks, 'If only someone weren't a bloody coward about bloody heights and had trained the bloody animals in the first place, they would have been bloody ready by now!'

'Michael!' Anka snaps sternly.

Katrina's face turns scarlet as she quickly lowers her head. Michael does not say anything else.

'Maybe we should take a break and consider our options,' you suggest.

The others nod. Katrina coughs lightly as she sits down on a rock. Gherk sits next to her, his giant apron rattling with pots and pans.

'It's, uh, OK, Katrina. We are, uh, all, uh, afraid of something. I'm, uh, afraid all the, uh, time.'

'There's a shocker,' Michael scoffs.

'Enough!' Talia shouts.

Michael rolls his eyes. 'I really hate you people sometimes.'

You notice how high his shoulders are, nearing his ears. You notice that his fists are turning white from him squeezing them so much. You can almost taste his anger.

Katrina, on the other hand, seems almost broken. Her eyes are devoid of emotion when she is listening to Gherk, and at other times she just lowers her gaze to the ground, as if she wishes she were in it.

It takes you a few moments but you recognise this: shame. Ever-consuming, like the world's most evolved virus, destroying anything in its passing. As you watch both Michael and Katrina struggling, you notice yourself starting to feel overwhelmed as well. There is so much painful emotion present all around you that you want to leave and come back when everyone feels better.

If you decide that you are going to leave until everyone calms down, go to page 123.

If you decide to support Michael and Katrina, go to page 53.

'Take my hand,' Anka says, extending her own wrinkly hand. 'Take it and ve go.'

Reluctantly, you take hold. You feel a pull. Then, it's as if your body is turning inside out and your head is floating separately from your body. You feel faint. Once again, you wonder if you are losing your mind.

Wind whooshes past your ears and only when it stops do you realise that you've instinctively closed your eyes. As Anka's hand pulls away, your feet hit what feels like a floor with an awkward thud, leading you to fall and stumble, hitting your right knee in the process.

'Oww,' you say as you open your eyes, rubbing your banged knee.

As you get up and look around you, you realise that you are in a peculiar house with Anka and six other strangers. The house seems to be located inside a massive tree trunk. Round painted windows allow the sunlight to seep inside as the moss-covered roots form the floor and the furniture. A wooden rocking chair in the back is shaped like a giant butterfly and a brown couch seems to be embedded in the tree and covered with sheep wool. Plants of different colours and sizes line the walls of the room, and a bowl of fresh oranges stands in the middle of a round wooden table in the centre.

A young red-haired woman, about nineteen or twenty, extends her hand.

'I'm Celeste. Come, meet the others,' she says, blinking her wide green eyes behind her glasses. Celeste points to the elf standing next to her. 'This is Lex, my roommate. Our house kind of became the headquarters for the legion.'

'Legion?' you ask.

'Yes, the Legion of Coeur. That's what we call ourselves.'

'So nice to meet you,' says Lex, who has shoulder-length black hair and wears a green shirt with matching trousers. Lex speaks with a slight accent. Japanese, maybe, if you had to guess.

'Would you like anything to drink?' Lex asks. 'I can make you—'

'Stop overwhelming our guest,' says a large, beautiful woman with long brown hair, wearing a long black dress. 'My name is Katrina. Welcome to Here.'

'Here?' you ask, still a bit disoriented by your trip. 'Where is here, exactly?'

'Uh-oh,' says Lex. 'Anka didn't explain Here to you?'

'Zere vas no time. Ze Strah came out of ze valls. Ve had to leave as soon as possible before zey returned.'

You feel everyone's gaze on you. One of the legion, a tall, dark, muscled man, approaches you. His face is stern, his lips pressed tight together as he looks you up and down, then turns to Anka.

'You took a big risk doing this,' he says. 'If the SAMs find out that we have a non-MESS Here, we will all be arrested and tortured.'

'I'm sorry, I don't quite understand what's happening,' you say.

'Michael, uh, stop scaring, uh, everyone,' says a giant grey ogre standing to your left. He barely fits in the room. The tuft of hair standing on top of his otherwise bald grey head touches the ceiling. Over his white shirt and dark trousers, he wears a long apron that reminds you of the wall of an enormous kitchen with many knives, pots and pans of different sizes hanging from it.

'Move, Gherk,' Michael snaps at the ogre, pushing past him. He takes a seat at a nearby table and types furiously on a laptop, his eyebrows furrowed.

'You have to, uh, forgive Michael,' says Gherk, wiping the spot on his shoulder that Michael ran into with a wet wipe. 'He, uh, works for the, uh, Magic Consulate—'

'Worked,' Michael corrects him.

'Ah, yes. Uh, forgive me. He, uh, worked for the consulate and he is, uh, worried that you, uh, may be, uh, tracked.'

'He can't help it. It's his training. He used to run Special Ops for the Consulate Military in the Dark Magic War,' says a dark-haired gothic girl, who wears a black spider-web dress. She's not any older than eighteen, you think. She extends her hand to you.

'I'm Talia,' she says. Small fangs in her mouth are visible as she gives you a gentle smile.

You introduce yourself, shaking her cold ghostly-white hand.

'No activity in the consulate,' Michael says as he closes the laptop. 'Yet. But that doesn't mean that we can afford to be complacent.' He then opens the table drawer and takes out a pamphlet, which he hands to you. 'This should explain things somewhat.'

You sit down at the table and read it, still aware that everyone in the room is staring at you. The pamphlet reads:

Welcome to Here, a world of the present moment. If you have arrived Here, it means that you have been able to openly and mindfully experience your emotions and are, in fact, a MESS – a Magically and Emotionally Sensitive Subject.

Once you find Here, you might start seeing it on maps and in many other aspects of your life. Here was created to help you embrace your MESS identity and bring out your unique gifts and magical abilities. These can include: witchcraft, healing, poetry, art, dancing, cosplaying and others.

Should you ever require guidance or additional information, please feel free to visit the Magic Consulate or contact one of our representatives.

Sincerely yours,
Mallena Phobian
Director of Magic Consulate

You read the letter several times before speaking.

'So, Here is where I am right now. And people who end up Here have been able to openly experience their emotions, and the goal of Here is to be OK with these emotions?' you ask.

'Basically, yes,' Talia replies.

'Including fear? Anxiety? Depression? All of that?' you ask her. 'Yes.'

'But . . . I don't want . . . I've never . . . I don't want to feel them!' A familiar sense of panic is settling in.

Michael narrows his eyebrows at you again. 'We know. And despite that, Anka thought it would be a good idea to bring you Here because she is convinced that you are the Chosen One.'

'Vhat vas I supposed to do? Let ze Strah destroy our only hope?'

'They were terrifying,' you say, trembling at the very memory of those dark, nasty mist creatures.

'Zat is vhat zey do. Zey scare you. Zey are not dangerous but enough of zem togezer can feel dangerous. In reality, zey just vant to stop you because zey work for Mallena.'

Your head begins to spin. 'But . . . why me?'

'That's actually what we all would like to find out,' Michael says, shooting you a disapproving gaze. Talia grunts at him.

'What does that mean?' you ask.

'It means—' Talia starts but Michael interrupts.

'We all know our special abilities,' he says. 'What is yours?'

You blush and grimace. 'Look . . . I'm sorry. I think you've got the wrong person. I don't have a special ability. I'm not—'

'Please,' says Gherk, tears welling in his eyes. 'People are, uh, disappearing. Others are, uh, losing their memories or, uh, becoming numb to the world. We, uh, need you. We need to, uh, bring them back.'

'For crying out loud, Gherk, she left you!' Michael shouts, grabbing the ogre by the shoulders. 'She couldn't take it any more and she's not coming back. End of story!'

As Michael lets go, Gherk sniffles. He then takes a wet wipe from his belt, wiping each shoulder ten times.

'Really? You're going to cry now? You're a man, for crying out loud!'

'And men aren't supposed to cry?' Lex asks.

'Exactly!'

'Who told you that?' Lex asks.

Michael opens his mouth. Then he closes it again and waves at the elf. 'Whatever.'

'Ignore him,' says Katrina to Gherk. She turns to you. 'Look, I understand that this is a lot of pressure for you, but Gherk is right. We do need you. According to Anka's prophecy, we have until the end of next Monday or . . .' she swallows, 'this world will no longer exist.'

Everyone is silent. You look at them staring at you and it's like the world has been put on pause.

'I . . . I don't . . .' you stumble over your words.

From outside, there's a cawing sound and then a rapping on the window. A large raven appears, knocking on the glass with its beak.

'Java!' Celeste cries as she runs to the window to open it.

The raven hops in and sits on her shoulder. He speaks in a deep but slightly muddled voice. 'They are coming. The SAMs are coming.'

Everyone looks alarmed.

'I told you this would happen!' Michael shouts at Anka, banging his fist on the table. He then turns to you. 'This is all *your* fault!'

Is he right? He must be right. He knows this world and its rules. You don't, you're an intruder, someone who came here without understanding why or how. You feel your feet going numb and your knees readying to give out.

'I . . .' you begin, unsure how to finish that sentence.

'Stop it, Michael,' Celeste snaps angrily. As Michael turns away from you, she takes a big gulp from a ceramic coffee mug with a picture of a raven on it. Around the picture, the mug reads in a circular fashion: *Self-Refilling Café Noir*. After she's done drinking,

Celeste licks her lips and takes a deep breath before she speaks to you. 'The SAMs are most likely going to inspect our MESS marks. We need to make sure you have one.'

You feel yourself both nervous and also intrigued. 'Who are SAMs? And what are MESS marks?'

'SAMs are the Special Agents of Magic,' Katrina explains calmly but quickly. 'They work for the consulate, so they ultimately answer to Mallena. They must have sensed that there is a new arrival Here. Whenever a new MESS arrives Here, this symbol is supposed to appear on their non-dominant arm.'

She points to her left wrist and shows you what looks like a small tattoo resembling an upside-down teardrop or a small balloon. Underneath it in small letters are the words: *You ARE HERE.*

'This is a MESS mark,' Katrina explains.

'I don't have one,' you say. 'So . . . what are they going to do to me?'

'To us,' Michael corrects you. 'We would be guilty of not reporting a non-MESS. Best-case scenario, they erase our memories and send us back to our own worlds. However, given that you are supposed to be a direct threat to Mallena, I doubt that we will get such a kind treatment.'

'This was a terrible mistake,' you say.

'Our only choice is to make you a MESS,' says Celeste.

'How?' you ask.

'I vill show you,' Anka says. 'Sit. Sit down.'

You do as she asks and she continues.

'In order to become a MESS you need to notice your difficult emotions and be villing to experience zem, instead of fighting zem.'

You feel your own shoulders tense. Feel your difficult emotions? This is the opposite of everything you were ever taught. As far as you can remember, people have always taught you just the opposite – 'be happy', 'just don't think about it', 'get over it' or the exasperated, 'EverythingIsFineWhyCan'tYouJustBeHappyLike EveryoneElseWhatInTheWorldIsWrongWithYou'.

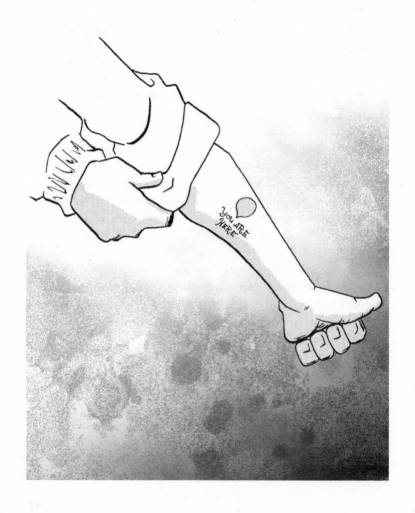

You stare at Anka and she stares back at you. Everyone else in the room watches and waits, almost as if you're expected to do a magic trick. If only you could make yourself disappear like a little bunny rabbit.

Is it too late to go home?

'How?' you ask. 'How do I do this?'

'We are doomed,' Talia groans.

'Don't give up, keep trying,' says Celeste.

Lex brings you a cup of warm tea. 'Maybe this will help.'

'Thanks,' you say as you take the cup and start gulping.

'Not like zat!' shouts Anka. 'Slowly. Drink very slowly and really taste ze tea.'

You take a slow sip, feeling the warmth spreading down your throat and into your chest. You focus on the raspberry flavour and the warmth of the cup in your hands. As you slow down your drinking, your heart and breathing slow down too. It's suddenly obvious how incredibly tense you've been. You take a breath and consciously relax your shoulders. Your anxiety is starting to reduce.

'Did it work?' you ask, rolling up both sleeves. Neither arm has the MESS mark.

'Apparently not,' Anka says. 'OK, close your eyes. Feel your feelings. Just feel zem.'

You close your eyes, frustrated and confused, two emotions that swirl inside and soon include embarrassment, as well as another feeling (maybe two?) that you can't quite name.

You open your eyes again. 'There, I felt them. That was horrible. Am I done now?'

'Let me see your arms,' Anka says.

Everyone stares as you once again inspect your arms and once again there is no MESS mark.

You look around at the alarmed looks on everyone's faces. Except Michael's. He looks furious . . . No. You know that it's not anger really but frustration. Maybe fear too. He probably worries about these people, worries that you are putting them in jeopardy.

There is a knock on the front door. Talia gasps and drops her teacup. Lex rushes to help her clean it up.

'Open up! Special Agents of Magic!' a gruff voice commands from the outside.

Lex opens the door and three tall men walk in. They are almost as tall as Gherk and nearly as wide. They have the bodies of men and the heads of bulls. Steam comes out of their nostrils when they exhale and their horns look sharp enough to pierce your body all the way through.

Minotaurs!

The tallest and the fiercest-looking of the three introduces himself. 'I'm Special Agent Hoffman of the Magic Consulate. These are my associates, Special Agent Abbott and Special Agent Capps.'

The agents behind him each grunt in acknowledgement. Hoffman turns toward Michael. 'Ellison – what are you doing here?'

Michael's shoulders visibly tense. 'I could ask you the same. I cannot believe you still work for her after—'

'We all do what we have to,' snaps Hoffman. He then turns to face the rest of the room. 'We need to see everyone's MESS marks.'

You close your eyes and prepare for the worst when . . .

'Frio!' shouts a familiar voice.

You open your eyes. Everyone except you and Celeste is frozen inside a hazy cloud of purple and silver.

'What's happened?' you ask.

'We have less than three minutes before the spell wears off,' she says, her voice rushed. She takes a big gulp of her self-refilling coffee, and then takes your hand in hers.

'Look,' she says to you, 'I know you are scared. I am too. We all are. We are all in this together.'

'OK. I just . . . I don't know what . . . It's almost like the more I try, the worse it gets.'

Celeste's eyes widen as she squeezes your hand. 'Say that last part again.'

'The more I try, the worse it gets?'

'That's it!' she says. 'Don't force it. Don't fight it. Just feel. Feel and know that you are a MESS. Please. Just . . . start by telling me how you feel right now.'

If you are willing to experience and talk about these vulnerable emotions, go to page 8.

If you are not willing to experience and talk about these emotions, go to page 158.

Leave Before You're Healed

Lose 5 inner strength and 5 wisdom points

You continue to suffer from the effects of the Fusion Potion and struggle to think clearly. This causes you to start doubting yourself and the legion. You feel ashamed and believe yourself to be completely and utterly inept in terms of completing this mission.

'Stupid idiot! What were you thinking?' you shame yourself. And then you feel angry. Angry at yourself for failing, at Anka for bringing you Here in the first place, angry at Mallena for starting this problem, angry at the whole world. You are never able to use the Moon Tradition properly, so whenever you encounter the Moon Tradition later in the story, you are not able to gain its benefits.

You separate from your group and wander in the forest by yourself, until you hear a rustling behind you. You barely get a chance to turn around when you are bitten by a werewolf.

Proceed to page 179.

You put down your piece of paper and collect yourself. Some of the others around you are sniffling or dabbing their eyes. Others simply look sombre. Gherk blows his nose, sounding a bit like a foghorn.

Gherk! You remember his name!

'Gherk!' you call to him. 'I remember you!'

He looks at you and, after a moment, smiles in recognition. 'I, uh, remember you too.'

Your stomach rumbles. 'How long have we been down Here?'

Michael checks his watch. 'An hour.'

You sigh with relief. 'OK, not too bad. We just need to find our exit and we'll be on our way.'

'No!' Michael shouts, jumping to his feet and looking at his watch in alarm. 'I just saw the date! We've been here for *twenty-five* hours!'

'*What?*' you and several others exclaim.

'We have less than twelve hours now,' Michael says, his eyes wide as he exhales. 'We need to split up and find the nearest exit immediately.'

'No,' Anka says. 'Ve stay togezer. If ve split up, ve are more likely to forget again.'

Michael turns to you. 'What should we do?'

You gulp and take a breath, noticing your own anxiety surge and then begin to fall again with each breath.

I can do this.

'OK,' you begin. 'We need to partner up. Each of us is responsible for our partner. We need to remember our core values: being a good friend, being courageous, helping others. We stay together in our group, next to our partners. Should you start having doubts about why you are Here, should you forget your purpose or want to give up, remember that you are Here for the legion. Remember that you are Here for your partner. Remember that you are Here to make the world a better place.'

'Couldn't have said it better myself,' Michael says. 'Katrina . . . if it's OK with you, I'd like you as my partner.'

Katrina blushes. 'Oh. Sure. And I'll guide the dragopurrs as well.'

All of you pair up: you with Anka, Lex with Talia, Michael with Katrina, Celeste with Gherk, and Blake with Eribelle. You look around. The misty water is hard to see through and everything beyond twenty or twenty-five feet seems dark and murky.

'Which way should we go?' Lex asks.

'Maybe ze direction in vhich ze fish are svimming?' Anka says.

You agree and set off after the fish, swimming placidly through the warm mists.

'Which direction are we going in?' you ask.

Michael looks at his smart watch. 'East.'

You continue for what seems like hours. Periodically, Anka grabs her chest and shouts, 'Gah!' Each time, you ask if she needs anything but she reassures you she's OK and walks ahead.

Your stomach growls and you consider asking Gherk to make you some food but think better of it. Every once in a while, Eribelle throws some fairy dust ahead to illuminate the way ahead but you still cannot see too far in front of you.

'How long have we been walking?' Blake asks.

Michael sighs. 'Four hours.'

'What's that?' you ask, pointing to a white, fluffy object near a stack of seaweed.

'That's Snowball!' Katrina shouts.

And indeed, you recognise the previously fuzzy and currently shabby-looking teddy bear. The dragopurrs run toward it excitedly, each tugging at its ears. Hektor yanks the bear away from

Hera and rolls on to his back, gently scratching the bear with his paws. Hera pounces on top of him, and the two felines roll around, each tugging at the teddy bear, pieces of white fuzz flowing around in the mists.

'Ve valked around in circle!' Anka shouts.

Michael cries out in anger and punches the air. Gherk collapses to his knees in defeat.

'What do we do now?' Katrina asks.

'Short on time, limited options,' Michael remarks. 'We just walked east to west. I suggest we try north to south.'

'And if we waste another four hours walking in a circle?' you ask.

'I'm open to suggestions,' he responds.

You look to Anka for guidance. She shrugs and says, 'I do not see any ozer choice. Eizer ve go nors or ve stay here and forget again. Ve have to do somesing.'

'I can lead,' Michael says, looking at his smart watch. 'North is that way.'

Hours later, you are still walking, more hungry and exhausted than you can ever remember feeling in the past. You find yourself wishing you could feel as calm and serene as you did when you first encountered the mists, just for a few minutes, even though it cost you your memory. Everyone around you looks tired and sullen. Even the dragopurrs blindly follow Katrina, no longer wrestling one another to the ground.

Just give up, a voice in your mind tells you. *'You'll never succeed at this. This is pointless.'*

No, you silently say back to your mind. *I have to keep going. For Anka. For Gherk. For Lex. For everyone Here. For the world of Here.*

'You are a fraud,' your mind responds.

I am having the thought that I am a fraud, you correct the voice. *Most people have that thought at some point. It means that I care about this mission and will do everything I can to succeed.*

You notice your tension reducing again as you silently continue with the Moon Tradition practices. *May we be safe. May I find the courage to face the things that scare me.*

You put your hands on your heart. Warmth spreads through your chest. At the same time, you look at Anka and you feel her pain in your own heart.

'What is this?' you ask Anka.

'Vhat is vhat?' she asks.

'What is this feeling of sadness that I feel when I can sense your pain while also feeling warmth in my heart?'

'Zis is compassion. Ze feeling of pain of anozer person is called empasy. It hurts you because you feel ze pain as if it is your own. But if you can connect viz your heart, as you are doing, you can experience empasy and love at ze same time. Zis is compassion.'

She stops walking suddenly and turns to you. 'You say you feel my pain?'

'Yes,' you say.

'Do you always feel ozer people's pain?'

'Well . . . I mean, not always. And not because I mean to. But . . . Yes. Most of the time, yes.'

'Hmm.'

'What is it?' you ask.

'I sink I am beginning to understand.'

'I figured. But understand what?'

'I believe zat—'

'Bloody hell! We are back to where we started again!' Michael shouts.

'So we basically just wasted another four hours?' Talia asks through gritted teeth.

'Five,' Michael says in a low voice. 'We've been walking at a much slower pace this time around.'

'Gah!' Anka gasps again, squeezing her chest as her heavy breaths give way to a coughing fit. Her eyes water and she spits out small drops of blood, causing some of the others to gasp in turn.

'Let me take a look at you,' Celeste says.

'No, no. It is OK,' Anka protests.

'You don't look good. Just let me take a look.'

'No! Ve must—' But she has another coughing fit, more blood now coming out of her mouth and trickling down her nose.

'Anka, please—' Celeste starts.

'No,' Anka says, pointing up with her finger. 'Ve have to go up.'

'Up?' you ask. 'But we couldn't—'

'Up,' Anka manages to say over the wheezing cough.

'Katrina—' Michael starts.

'Let's do it,' she responds in a firm voice. 'Everyone, mount the dragopurrs.'

You help Anka saddle in, supporting her body, which jerks and shivers from her coughing.

'I don't know that we'll be able to go up,' Blake says. 'The net—'

'Well, we have to try,' Katrina cuts him off.

Once you are all saddled, she yells, 'Up! *Up!*'

The dragopurrs lift up and take off. The felines seem insecure about this. Hektor rocks side-to-side, clearly struggling, while Hera is flying up slowly and cautiously.

'I think it's the mists,' Eribelle says. 'They are making everyone lethargic, and are probably making Anka sicker.'

'Not to mention the fact that we haven't slept or eaten in a long time,' Celeste says.

'Up!' Katrina shouts again as Hera begins to descend.

Anka's cough is getting more severe as the air gets heavier and becomes more difficult to breathe. Both felines are struggling now, descending a foot for every three that they rise.

'Iz . . . getting . . . heavier . . . Ve . . . have . . . to . . . go . . . up . . . fast . . .' Anka forces out in between horrendous coughs.

'We have to make a sharp push straight up,' Michael says to Katrina. 'Do you think the dragopurrs can do that?'

'I don't know. They've never done anything like this before and they're exhausted.'

'They need to or we all die here,' he says. 'And there's one more thing.'

'What?'

'If we manage to get up above the mists, we have to keep going higher. We can't afford to get caught in those nets again.'

'How much higher?' she asks cautiously.

'I don't know. Higher. A lot. It's our only chance.'

Katrina gulps. Michael looks at her sympathetically and his voice softens as he says, 'I know that you are scared. We all are. But you can do it. I believe in you.'

Katrina takes a breath. 'OK. I'm going to follow my core values . . . even though I am afraid.'

'There you go!' Michael smiles at her.

'Everyone, hold on! Up! *Up! UUUPPP!*' she shouts.

The dragopurrs kick off once more and shoot straight up, lifting higher and higher. The pressure pushes against you, but the higher they get, the easier it is for them to fly. You smile at this, feeling hopeful, then see that Anka is still coughing, her hands now covered in blood.

'Hang on,' you tell her. 'We're almost there.'

A few more feline jumps and finally, you are above the mists. You can breathe again and you feel everyone's relief.

'Great job!' Michael says to Katrina. 'Now keep them going up.'

'I don't know . . .' Katrina's voice is shaky.

'You can do it. Remember what it's all for.'

'For you,' she says. 'For all of us Here. OK. Up! Up! *Up!*'

The dragopurrs climb up through the chill night air. Straight ahead, through looming clouds, you can see the grotesque outline of the gloomy castle partially illuminated by the moonlight.

'You are doing so well!' Michael says, rubbing Katrina's shoulder. 'OK, now let's try to land on top of that tower.'

Katrina looks tense, her jaw and fists clenched. Despite this, she guides the felines to the top of the tower. A few minutes later, the dragopurrs gently land there.

'Great job!' Michael says to Katrina.

'I did it!' she whispers. Then she squeals, 'I did it! I actually did it!'

'I never doubted that you could.' He smiles. He seems about to add something, but Katrina suddenly squeezes him in a tight hug and then plants a big kiss on his lips.

Meanwhile, you help Gherk and Blake bring Anka down to the tower. She is wheezing and shaking, but the coughing has stopped. You sit next to her and cradle her head in your arms as Celeste begins to summon her magic.

'Don't . . .' Anka says to her, her voice barely audible, her speech and breathing highly laboured. 'It vill . . . not help now . . .' She coughs again. 'You vill have to let me go.'

No one says a word. The silence is harsher than a freshly sharpened knife. Your chest feels heavy and your eyes burn.

Anka motions for you to get closer so that your ear is next to her mouth. 'I know,' she says in a soft whisper. 'I know vhy you are ze Chosen One.'

You lift your head to look at her. 'Why?'

She pulls you close to her again and whispers, 'You are empat . . . Like Mallena.'

Empath? You have always known you could empathise with others but is that a good enough reason?

'Anka, even if I am an empath, why does that make me the Chosen One?'

'Because . . . you . . . can feel . . . her heart . . .' A single tear runs down her face. She takes your hand and you feel what she's feeling. You start to sob unexpectedly and a moment later you know why.

'Don't go,' you say to her. 'Don't.'

'I vill not . . . not really . . . Remember zat,' she says. She then points to your heart and continues, 'If you ever . . . need me . . . I vill always be . . . right Here . . .'

You feel every emotion but cannot name a single one. Everything blurs. Anka's hand drops. Her eyes close and she stops moving. A moment passes, then another, and you realise you can't feel her emotions any more. You try to shake her awake but nothing happens.

'Anka! Anka! Please!'

No response. You sob again, feeling the legion members around you, feeling some of their hands on your shoulders, offering you comfort. Before you can say anything, a familiar voice intrudes.

'Turn around and raise your hands up!'

You jump to your feet and whirl around. Hoffman is standing there with a group of Minotaurs.

Proceed to page 10.

Emotional Numbing

Lose 4 inner strength points

Similar to experiential avoidance (the opposite of acceptance), emotional numbing refers to choosing to turn away from one's emotions and being inauthentic. While numbing your emotions might allow you to guard yourself from getting hurt, it might also prevent you from experiencing happiness.

For example, if you never make any friends, you will never be hurt or betrayed by a friend. However, you will also miss out on potentially amazing experiences and excellent adventures.

The truth is that we cannot selectively numb our emotions. We cannot experience happiness if we are not open to experiencing sadness, and we cannot feel love if we are unwilling to experience a potential heartbreak. Not really. Of course, you might love someone but be unwilling to try connecting with them due to potential heartbreak. However, in that case, we miss out by default and are guaranteed to never have a meaningful connection with that individual.

At the end of their lives most people tend to regret not the things they did, not the setbacks they had, but the chances they didn't take, the missed opportunities to be vulnerable and to connect with others.

Turn to page 76 to continue your quest.

You realise that the mist monsters are gone. Completely gone. You breathe with relief.

'Come viz me if you vant to live.'

You look up at the voice from above and see a woman in a long white dress, embroidered with black and red stitching. She has wrinkles on her face and smells of sour cream and cabbage. She looks intense.

'Who . . . who are you?' you ask. 'Where did you come from? And what were those things that attacked me?'

'My, my. Zat is many kvestions,' she says, helping you up on to your feet. 'My name is Anka. Ve vill need to go before zey come back.'

'Who are they?' you ask.

'Ze Strah,' she replies with a shudder in her voice. 'Zat is vat zey are called, zose creatures zat attacked you. Zey feed on fear and try to keep you from living meaningful life.'

'What do they want from me?'

'To scare you. To keep you from your mission.'

'What mission?' you ask.

'To help stop magical sorceress from destroying ze vorld.'

You stare at Anka for a moment, wondering if she is playing a trick on you. What she said is silly, but then again you did just fight those horrid monsters. As you ponder how to reply, her face remains serious and unmoving.

You finally utter, 'Ma'am, I don't know who you are or why you're here, but I'm certain you have the wrong person.'

159

She sighs. 'Zey never believe me.'

'Who's they?' you ask, frustrated by her cryptic answers.

'Zey. You know. People. Zey never believe psychics.'

You raise your eyebrows. 'Psychics?'

She takes a step closer. Her long white dress flares with red and black stitching, matching the red and black bands in her waist-long plait.

'You are ze only one who can possibly stop her.'

'Stop who?'

'Mallena. Ze sorceress from our vorld. I have a vision about it. Our vorld vill end in seven days if Mallena is not stopped and you are ze only one who can stop her.'

'You had a vision that I stop—'

'Possibly stop,' she corrects.

'Possibly stop an evil sorceress from destroying another world?'

'Yes,' she answers.

'And how exactly am I supposed to be able to do that?'

'Zat I do not know.'

Your shoulders tense in frustration.

'Well, then what do you know?' you spit out in anger.

'I know a lot. I know zat you are person who iz afraid zat if people really get to know you, zey vill not like you. You often feel like you do not belong in zis vorld. You often feel lonely, even vhen you are around ozer people. You often vish you could be a hero but believe yourself to be too scared to do anysing heroic. You often vish you could be part of somesing magical. You have a lot of fear – being loved, being rejected, living your life vizout finding meaning . . . Am I on ze right track? I see by your face zat I am at least very close. Ultimately, you vill have to make choices.'

'What choices?' you ask.

'Choices about everysing. Deciding if you go on ze mission, deciding how you proceed . . .'

'What if I make the wrong choice?'

'Zen you will face ze consequences.'

You gulp and stare at Anka.

'Here is your first choice: you can come viz me and start your mission, or stay here and go back to sleep.'

If you choose to stay at home and go back to sleep, go to page 90.

If you choose to accept Anka's invitation to go on this quest, go to page 9.

You grab the choker and throw it on the floor, shouting, 'I'm not ever putting that on!'

Mallena stares at you in silence for a moment. Then she smiles, but her smile never reaches her eyes.

'We'll see,' she says. She then turns to Hoffman and says, with a hint of sarcasm, 'Let's reunite our *hero* with the others.'

Hoffman bows before grabbing your arms. He escorts you out of the interrogation room, down the filthy corridor, and into a slightly larger cell, where you see the rest of the legion members. He opens the cell door, jams you in, and thrusts the choker into your hands.

'You'll need it,' he says and walks off. As soon as he's out of sight, Talia runs up to you.

'Oh, thank God!' she exclaims. 'Are you OK? We all thought you were dead.'

'Not quite,' you respond and tell them about what happened.

Gherk picks up the choker and inspects it. 'So this, uh, will, uh, help, uh, take away, uh, my pain?'

Anka shakes her head. 'Not exactly. I believe zat it vill numb your emotions but zat it vill make you suffer in ozer vays.'

Gherk looks up at her, devastated, his bottom lip trembling. He looks older, somehow, as he says, 'I, uh, cannot, uh, do this, uh, any more.' With that, he lowers his head in shame.

'Gherk, no!' Lex screams, wresting the choker out of the ogre's hands. 'You were about to put that on!'

'I . . . uh . . . can't . . .' Gherk falls to his knees and weeps.

'Oh, geez, Gherk!' Michael shouts at him. 'You're a man! Stop it!'

Gherk looks up at him, tears still rolling down his cheeks, as Michael continues to yell at him.

'Stop crying! You're a man, for crying out loud! Stop it!'

'You're doing it again,' Lex says. 'Seriously, whose words are those?'

'What?'

'You keep shaming him for crying. I was just wondering, who told you that men shouldn't cry?'

Michael looks dumbfounded. 'Look, I know you elves are high and mighty with your uni-gender, so I don't expect *you* to understand, but—'

'Answer the question, Michael,' Lex says. 'Who told you?'

Michael's face changes from anger to slow contemplation. He lowers his head and then looks up again, confused. 'I don't know. Different people? I guess . . . my father.'

There is silence in the room as everyone looks at Michael as he continues. 'He'd always tell me that real men don't cry . . .' He closes his eyes. 'He shamed me for crying when my dog died . . . He beat me for crying when my mum died . . . I was six . . . And if I ever cried when he was hitting me . . . he'd hit me . . . until I stopped.'

Gherk sniffles and puts his enormous arm around Michael. Michael lowers his head and sobs.

You lower your head, your own eyes tearing up, your own memories of being shamed for your emotional experiences replaying at an excruciatingly slow pace, every detail highlighted in your mind. You remember every word, every moment when you so badly wanted to have someone understand you, to support you, reassure you, to tell you that everything would be OK. And instead you were shamed for how you felt. You were told to 'stop taking things so personally' and 'stop being so sensitive'.

You remember every heartbreak, every moment that you held your breath to see if you would hear back from the one person who really mattered, waited to find out if they still loved you, waited to find out if they were still in your life. You remember every time you shamed yourself for how scared, insecure, jealous, angry, anxious, depressed or hopelessly unloved you felt. You remember being shamed for caring too much about what other people think or were devastated about a tragedy that involved people you've never met.

'Why do you care?' someone would ask you. 'You don't even know them.'

Didn't they know that your heart was breaking, that the pain of others somehow became your own?

Overwhelmed by these memories and emotions, you contemplate putting on the choker again, when Talia suddenly covers her ears and shouts, 'These voices! Make them stop!'

'What voices?' you ask her.

'It feels like a soundtrack that's being broadcast directly into my mind. It's awful. Make it stop!'

'Wait! Did any of you eat anything since we've been captured?' you ask.

'No, they didn't exactly roll out the feast for us. We're not the Chosen Ones,' Michael says, sarcasm returning to his voice.

'Water!' Celeste realises. 'We all drank water.'

You look around at each other.

'So that Fusion garbage is now happening to us?' Michael asks.

'I think so,' you say, feeling both guilty and scared. 'But we can stop it.'

You explain the Defusion antidote to the group, and in a few moments everyone is practising, filling the room with overlapping murmurs.

'I'm having a thought that I'm a failure, I'm having a thought that I'm a coward, I'm having a thought that I'm not a real man, I'm having a thought that I am weak and broken . . .' Michael practises.

'I believe zat being in zis room is making it harder for us to practise. I believe ze cell is affected too,' Anka says, grabbing her chest.

'Let me try something,' Celeste says and takes a large gulp of her coffee.

She then stands in the middle of the cell and closes her eyes. She begins whispering something you cannot make out, drawing a field of magic in the air with her hands. Soon purple and silver sparks begin to fly out of her hands. The air in the room vibrates as her whispering grows louder.

'Aaah!' She falls to her knees, covering her head with her arms.

Anka and Lex rush over to her. 'Your magic vill not vork here. Ze room is cursed. You just rest now.'

'No,' Celeste says, her speech slurred. 'I have to try again.'

'No . . . It is too dangerous,' Anka says, holding Celeste's shoulder with one hand and her own chest with another.

'Anka is right, Celeste. You already have a migraine. You don't need to kill yourself in the process. It's of no use to . . .' Lex tries to convince her.

'I . . . have . . . to . . .' Celeste says, rising back up.

She spreads her arms out once more and, with a loud groan, emits a cloud of silvery-purple dust from her hands, which blankets the cell and everyone in it. Celeste collapses on the ground, her nose bleeding and her body twitching.

You feel as if you've just been given oxygen after nearly suffocating under water. The voices in your head are not as loud as they were and your emotions settle enough for you to function. You shake your head to shake off the remaining fog of your internal thoughts and help Lex and Anka carry Celeste to one of the beds.

After a few moments, she stops shaking and then slowly opens her eyes. She groans from pain, tears rolling down her face, and she closes her eyes again.

'Is she, uh, OK?' Gherk asks.

'She uses her body's energy to fuel her healing magic,' Lex explains. 'Like most in the healing arts, she rarely uses it to restore her own functioning. Draining herself causes a lot of pain.'

'Why does she do that to herself?' Michael asks.

Celeste slowly opens her eyes. Her eyes are red, blood vessels have popped in both of them from the pressure, and a single tear is running down her left cheek. 'Because if I try hard enough, then maybe people will love me,' she says, before losing consciousness.

Everyone is silent. A few moments later, there's a slight noise behind you, as if someone is choking. You turn around in time to see Talia hit the ground with a thud.

'Talia!' Lex screams and you both run over. Talia is lying on her stomach, twitching. You shake her.

'Talia! Talia! Are you OK?'

She doesn't answer. You roll her over. Her eyes are closed, a thin silver choker blinking red around her neck.

Proceed to page 81.

Lack of Present Moment Awareness

Lose 3 wisdom points

The hags carry you away from your mission and keep you trapped in the pain of your past and in the fear of your future. Staying stuck in the past does not help you because you cannot change it. Spending all your time worrying about the future may also not be helpful. While some future planning might help you to be more prepared to face some obstacles, getting carried away by the potential future catastrophes is likely to keep you stuck.

To *catastrophise* is to imagine worst-case scenarios and live them out in your mind. When you do this, you don't focus on the present moment, where you are actually safe, where these tragic things are not occurring.

Your mind is great at catastrophising. In fact, it can be quite creative, writing out terrible stories in your mind that would put many horror movies to shame. However, your catastrophising mind might not be accurate. Think about it: how many times in your life have you imagined that something terrible or very embarrassing would happen? Chances are that those numbers are in the millions. And how many times have those terrible things actually occurred? Probably very rarely. This means that your mind is not psychic, though it might pretend to be, which in turn suggests that you cannot take the future-based thoughts that it creates as facts. The only thing that is real is the present moment.

When you are ready to get unstuck, proceed to page 69 but don't collect any points.

Eribelle shouts the instructions: 'First step: notice your thoughts and your sensations.'

You close your eyes and feel your anxiety. You notice yourself feeling tense and nervous. You take a breath. *I am noticing my feelings of anxiety. I am having the thought that I am a fraud and that I am a failure.*

Mallena casts the Faceless hags, who try to grab you, sending horrifying images of all the legion members wearing the chokers into your mind.

'Stay present!' Eribelle reminds all of you.

You take a breath and look at your MESS mark. *You are HERE.* Your mind shifts back into focus as you connect with the present moment.

'Remember all those times you've messed up in the past, like that one time . . .' one of the Faceless begins.

For a moment your mind cycles through all your least favourite memories, but you again willingly bring your mind to the present moment as a white cloud begins to form around you. One by one the Faceless begin popping off until none are left.

'Great job, everyone!' Eribelle says. 'Now step two—'

But she doesn't get to finish because Mallena's spell throws her into the wall, knocking her out.

You take a breath. It's up to you now. 'Next step is Common Humanity!' you instruct the legion.

I'm not alone in feeling this way. Most people struggle with self-doubt, you think to yourself.

As you practise, the silver cloud around you grows denser and the black one grows thinner.

'You're all doing great!' you encourage the others. 'Now the last step: Loving Kindness for ourselves and others.'

You all put your hands on your hearts. You begin to recite the Loving Kindness phrases, first for yourself:

'May I be happy. May I be free from pain and suffering . . .'

As you feel your own heart open enough to help others, you focus and send the compassionate wishes to everyone in the room.

'May you all know how loved you are. May you know how much you matter . . .'

CRACK!

You all turn in the direction of the noise and see Hoffman holding two pieces of the choker in his hands.

'What have you done?' Mallena shouts at him.

'I thought that not feeling the pain of my wife's illness was the best way that I could help her. I was wrong. This is.' And with those words he joins the circle, standing between you and Katrina and asking, 'How can I help?'

Celeste teaches him the Loving Kindness phrases and Hoffman places his enormous hands on his heart and adds his voice to the Moon Tradition practice. The silver cloud now fully blankets the thin remainder of the black cloud, until the latter dissipates completely. The silver cloud slowly fades as well, revealing the smiling faces of those standing in the circle.

'TRAITOR!' Mallena shouts at Hoffman. 'How could you?'

Hoffman lowers his enormous head in shame. 'I'm sorry, Mallena. But this was the right thing to do.'

'We'll see,' she spits out. 'When I'm done with you, you'll be begging me for another one.'

She waves her arms frantically in the air and a large swarm of dark figures materialise out of her fingertips.

'The Strah!' you and Hoffman cry out at the same time.

'We can't defeat them!' Hoffman says.

'We can,' you say.

Everyone looks at you, surprised.

'I figured it out,' you explain. 'Remember the Mists?'

'You were trapped in the Mists of Complacency?' Hoffman asks, impressed. 'And you survived?'

'Obviously,' you say. 'The Mists made us forget ourselves. We only got out of there because we were able to remember and connect with our core values.'

'What are you saying?' Michael asks.

'The Strah are basically our biggest fears keeping us from connecting with our core values. To stop them, we have to face them and do the opposite of what they tell us.'

'As you say, captain,' Michael says. 'But you're going to have to tell us what to do.'

'OK, but I don't actually know what I am doing,' you admit, blushing with embarrassment.

'*FRAUD! YOU ARE A FRAUD!*' the Strah hiss like a loud storm. '*YOU SHOULD JUST GIVE UP RIGHT NOW!*'

If you choose to listen to the Strah and give up right now, continue to page 176.

If you choose to face the Strah, despite your fear, proceed to page 178.

As the night preparations begin, chilling thoughts enter your mind. *What if I fail? What if someone gets killed? What if I get killed?*

You look down at your MESS mark. *You are HERE.* You take a breath. *My feet are on the ground and I am Here.* You place your hands on your heart and breathe. *I'm having a thought that I'm a fraud. I'm having a thought that we are in danger. Most people in this situation would have these thoughts. Everyone Here is probably having these thoughts right now.* You take a few more breaths. *May we be safe. May we be happy. May we—*

A loud sound of an explosion interrupts your ritual. You are up on your feet now, as is everyone else. The dragopurrs hiss and fly up into the air.

'What was that?' you ask.

'Explosive arrow,' Michael says, turning to face everyone else. 'We are under attack! OK, Celeste, Eribelle and Anka, I need you to set traps; the rest of you, come with me!'

You follow Michael as you overhear Anka giving instructions to Celeste and Eribelle: 'Tie ze loop. Attach ze peg. Good. Tilt it forty-five degrees . . .'

You hear the sounds of magic as Celeste and Eribelle follow Anka's instructions.

You help Michael stacking up branches as Gherk, Blake, Lex and Talia work on ripping the trees from the ground and binding them with magic in order to create a wall to fortify the territory.

You hear a familiar booming voice sounding over a bullhorn. You recognise the voice as Agent Hoffman's. 'You are surrounded. Come out with your hands up.'

'Not a chance!' Michael yells back.

'Last warning,' Hoffman says.

'Bite me, Hoffman!'

'ATTACK!' Hoffman shouts.

You see at least two dozen Minotaurs charging toward your legion, their horns gleaming in the moonlight. Four of them fall into a leaf-covered ditch that Anka and Eribelle set up, stumbling over each other almost comically. Now aware of the trap, the rest of the Minotaurs run around it. Three more trip over a wire and get knocked out by the pulley system Anka and Celeste prepared.

Java flies high above, cawing with updates: 'About fifteen more incoming.'

The remaining Minotaurs charge at the rest of you. Gherk, refusing to use his kitchen knives in battle, defends himself and others with giant pots and pans. In the meantime, Michael is fighting two of them in hand-to-hand combat as you and Lex team up against two more. Celeste manages to temporarily turn one of them to stone and then ties him to a tree, while Blake is fighting two others. As you look over, you see Gherk has managed to knock out four SAMs by himself while Eribelle has frozen three of them.

There's a whistling sound and Katrina directs the dragopurrs toward the SAMs. 'Ready? Fire!'

The felines fly up and breathe fire in the direction of the Minotaurs. Most of them take off running before the jets of flame can catch them.

'Come back! Cowards!' Hoffman shouts, now trapped in one of Eribelle's golden nets.

'How embarrassing,' says Java. 'How many Minotaurs does it take to lose a battle? Do you know? I'll tell you. It's—'

A scarlet arrow with a neon head flies from the direction of the Minotaurs. There seems to be all the time in the world to stop it

and yet there is no time at all before it reaches its target. In the same moment, the raven's eyes widen with shock as Celeste's face drains pale with horror. The next second, she falls to her knees, weeping, as Java takes his last breath.

Full of rage, you look up but most of the Minotaurs have disappeared.

Proceed to page 110.

Inaction

Lose all your points

The Strah take over your life and the lives of your friends. The world of Here is destroyed and you are stuck living in your feared future.

Go back to page 1.

Identity Constant

Gain 10 wisdom points

This must have been a very hard choice to make. It's not easy to accept what happens to us as a part of ourselves without becoming overly identified with the new sense of identity. Throughout our lives we go through many changes. Some are exciting, such as graduations, friendships and opportunities. And others can be difficult, such as heartbreaks, setbacks and disappointments. Though you might change in some ways, who you are isn't what happens to you.

You are someone who experienced these things, both the exciting and the difficult times, and you are also so much more than that. You are what you stand for, you are what you believe in, and you are a combination of your hobbies, strengths and desires. You are like a mountain, an unmoving symbol of ultimate power and foundation. And even when there is a storm and some of the pebbles and shrubbery on your surface have shifted, you are still that mountain.

You are still you. Someone who can observe the changes as they occur, including the depressive moments, the fears and anxieties brought on by the Faceless or the Strah, or any werewolf transformations. Underneath it all, you are still you.

Take a moment to observe the changes in your mind and in your body as if you were viewing them on a television screen, as if they are happening to someone else. Just notice whatever thoughts and experiences you have. And notice yourself noticing these. Take a breath. You are not a werewolf. You are a mountain of strength.

Proceed to page 100.

Committed Action

*Gain courage, wisdom and inner strength. These
are no longer game points. These are your actual
strengths and they stay with you. Always.*

Facing our own deepest fears is one of the hardest things we can
ever do. In particular, when our own internal self-critic tells us
that we are going to fail or that we are not good enough, we often
believe these voices to be true. Too often we allow these internal
fears to hold us back from doing what is really important to us,
from following our mission, our core values. As you might remember, committed action refers to taking specific steps to honour
your core values. For example, if you value being a good friend to
others, a committed action might include calling or texting your
friend. If you value creativity, your committed actions might
include drawing, painting, writing, cosplaying and others.

Under normal circumstances, making committed actions
might seem intimidating and make you feel vulnerable. When
faced with your own insecurities and homicidal sorcerers, committed actions might be even harder to make. Remember that it is
perfectly OK for you to feel afraid, insecure, depressed or uncomfortable. Any emotion is fair game. However, your emotions don't
have to hold you back from doing what's really important to you.
Be afraid, be nervous, be insecure, scream, cry if you need to, and
do the right thing anyway.

Proceed to page 190.

The light of the morning sun hits your eyelids as you struggle to open them. Your right shoulder feels as if a serrated dagger is piercing it over and over again. Your vision is still blurry, but you hear faint, familiar voices around you.

'Make sure that you apply the white magic to yourself first before using the healing spell.'

'Yes, yes, I know, Eribelle, but we have to stop the bleeding.'

Someone's gentle hands put pressure on your shoulder. Your shoulder feels almost completely numb, accompanied with prickles and tickles. You try to move the fingers of your right hand but they do not seem to be cooperating.

You slowly squint your eyes open, first the left, then the right.

'You're awake.' Celeste smiles and takes a large gulp of her coffee. She looks pale but does not seem to be in distress at the moment. 'We were all so worried.'

You try to sit up but the pain in your shoulder is so sharp that you scream and fall back down, tears forming in your eyes from the agony you feel.

'Shh, shh. Best if you don't try to get up right now,' says Celeste.

You groan, close your eyes and pass out again. When you open your eyes again, the pain is mostly gone, only a shadow of what it was. You wiggle your fingers. Then your wrist. Then your entire arm.

It works.

You slowly lift yourself up and look around. You are propped up against a tree, a few feet away from where you were attacked.

The rest of the legion are sitting in a circle a few feet away and talking in hushed voices. Michael is the first to notice you.

'You're awake.'

Celeste and Eribelle rush over to you.

'How are you feeling?' Eribelle asks.

'Umm . . . OK . . . I guess,' you say, your mind in a fog.

'How's your shoulder?' Celeste asks.

'Better. Thanks.'

You try to lift yourself up but are still too weak. You collapse back down.

'You shouldn't be—' Eribelle starts.

'I want to get up,' you insist.

'Here, let me help you,' Celeste says and puts your left arm around her as you lift yourself off the ground.

You are still feeling lightheaded, swaying from side to side. You lean your back against the tree, Celeste still holding you up by your left arm.

'How are you feeling?' an unfamiliar voice asks.

You turn your head in the direction of the voice and see a very tall, thin man wearing a pink suit and pink glasses. For a moment, you wonder whether you are hallucinating.

'W-w-who . . . are . . . you?' you're finally able to ask.

'This is my friend, Blake,' Eribelle speaks for him. 'He's the neuroscientist I was telling you about.'

Blake extends his long, skinny arm to you. 'Hi. Pleasure. So sorry about the . . . the bite . . . I thought . . .'

You pull your hand away mid-shake. 'You? You bit me?' You feel anger pulsating through your veins, adrenaline pumping through your body.

Blake lowers his head apologetically, placing his right hand on his chest. 'Yes. I'm . . . so sorry. I really thought you were one of those . . . exterminators.'

'Exterminators?' you ask.

'Oh, um . . . Yes. I guess you're new Here. Imps have been organising all over the world in their hatred of everything that's different from them, but specifically minorities, like my kind – werewolves. They also don't like ogres, witches or giants, but werewolves are their favourite targets.'

'How is that allowed?' you ask.

'It wasn't. The truth is that the imps were always a hateful kind, but ever since Mallena's changed regime, they've become more vocal. They've started forming gangs and teaming up with the Minotaurs in killing our kind and washing their white hats in our blood. "Redcaps", we call them, the imps.'

'You still had no right to bite me. You had no reason to think I was one of those . . . imps.'

'You're right. I have no excuses. I felt threatened and I reacted without thinking. Please forgive me.'

Although logically you know that the situation was an unfortunate accident, you still struggle to control your anger. Nearly falling over with dizziness, you look at him and shout, 'I don't care about your reasons. Just get away from me! Get lost!'

'That's enough!' Lex says.

'That's OK,' Blake responds. 'It can't be helped. When someone starts transforming, they often struggle with managing their emotions. Adrenaline can overtake their body, causing a massive fight-or-flight response. This can trigger feelings of anger, fear or despair.'

You start seeing red, as if your world is placed in a red filter. You see red trees, red people, red, red, red . . . Your heart is pounding. All you want to do is scream, or hit someone. Or bite someone and never let go of your grip. As if sensing this, Blake puts his hand on your shoulder.

'I'm so sorry . . .'

You throw his hand off. 'Don't touch me! Just . . . get away from me!'

He raises up both hands, as if to say that he will not argue, and slowly backs away. You slide down the base of the tree and growl at Celeste to keep her distance.

'Oh, terrific!' Lex snaps. 'We have two days left to stop Mallena and now we are fighting and turning into werewolves!'

You give a nasty look to the red-looking elf. 'Hey! You are not the one turning into a bloody werewolf! If you're in such a hurry, then go on without me!'

'Maybe we should!' Lex fires back and then turns to Michael. 'C'mon, Michael, let's go.'

Michael doesn't move. Lex looks at him, visibly furious.

'Are you bloody kidding? You've been saying this entire time that we need to head to the castle! And now that you have someone willing to follow you, you're staying behind?'

Michael looks down and then back up at Lex. He sighs and then speaks, choosing his words carefully. 'Lex, I was wrong. We need to stay together and we need to think this through . . .'

'Fine! So in the meantime, we can just sit Here, watch Talia die, watch the *Chosen One* become a bloody werewolf, until . . . what? Until it magically comes to us how to break the bloody choker?'

'Stop shouting!' you snap.

Lex turns toward you sharply. You're ready to strike, if needed, and you know that it would not end well.

'Lex!' Blake calls. 'I'm trying to figure out how the choker works, so that we can remove it from Talia. Can I ask for your assistance?'

Lex grunts at you and then follows Blake away toward the tree stump where Talia is sitting. Everyone else follows them, with the exception of Anka, who sits under the maple tree next to you. You sneer at her but hold your tongue.

Oh, great! Now she's going to tell me to accept it, to find some silver lining in this. You feel your shoulders tense, ready to snap at her at the very mention of it, waiting for her to lecture you about your behaviour and your attitude.

But she doesn't. She says nothing at all. She puts her hands on her heart and breathes at the same pace with you. After a few minutes, you notice that your breathing is slowing down, as is hers. A few more minutes and your muscle tension begins to decrease, and you start feeling a sense of relief. You are no longer seeing the world through a red filter and are starting to feel more like your old self.

'Thanks,' you say.

'For vhat?'

'For not saying anything.'

'I have nosing zat I can say zat vill make you feel better. I vish I could. But I cannot.'

Your eyes well up with tears as you realise how badly you needed to hear those words, how badly you wanted someone to just understand you in this way.

'Thanks,' you say again.

'You know, I do not believe I ever told you zat I used to vork as engineer in Ukraine.'

You look at her, unsure of where this is going. 'No, Anka. You never told me.'

'Yes. I vas engineer and zen I vas invited to vork in ze United States on big research grant. I used to vork every day. Veekends, holidays. I used to vork all ze time. And it vas very good research and ve got more and more funding.'

'Why are you telling me this?'

'Because one day I felt very bad pain in my left breast. I vent to ze doctor and ze doctor said zat I have stage-four breast cancer, less zan twenty-five per cent chance of survival . . .'

You sit up and stare at her, feeling your own heart twinge. 'Is this why you often grab your chest?'

'Yes.'

'How did you heal?'

'I did not,' she replies, and you feel shivers all over your body. 'Ze doctors said that treatment vould only extend my life little bit. I chose not to.'

You stare at her, unsure how to respond, as she continues. 'I vas devastated. Zere vas nosing anyone could say to make me feel better. Some people vould try. Zey vould say, "Don't vorry, it is for ze best" or "At least you still have some time left", but zeir efforts to cheer me up only made me more upset. I vould come home and cry. And my hedgehog, Yozhik, he vould just breeze viz me. And it vas ze only comfort I had. No one to tell me to feel any different. Just someone to breeze viz me.'

You smile at her, understanding.

'I know I am no hedgehog but I understand ze power of taking away ze pressure to say ze right sing or ze pressure to "fix it", and to just breeze viz someone else.'

Your heart is warmer now as the anger is completely gone. Left in you instead is sadness, fear and devastation.

'I . . . just . . . I don't want this, Anka. I don't want to be a werewolf.'

'I understand,' she says. 'I did not vant my affliction eizer.'

'How did you cope?'

'I reminded myself zat I am not my cancer.'

'Huh?' you ask, confused.

'I am not my cancer. I am someone viz cancer, but I am also so many ozer sings. I am someone who loves animals, especially my hedgehog. I am engineer. I am researcher. I am voman. And I am psychic too.'

'So what did you do?'

'I kvit my job at ze laboratory and I started living. I spent time viz myself, viz my hedgehog. I spent time eating good food and being around good people. I spent time in nature, constantly reminding myself zat I am not my cancer.' She leans closer to you. 'And you are not verevolf.'

'But . . . I've been bitten. I'm—'

'Yes. You vere bitten. And you vill probably have changes and transformations, vhich vill be hard for you. As I can see, you have two choices: you can become verevolf and let zis new identity consume you. Or you can be you, someone who is scared, someone who has doubts, someone who sometimes struggles viz lycansropy, or depression, or anxiety, but someone who knows vhat you stand for.'

If you choose to become a werewolf, go to page 27.

If you choose to connect with yourself while acknowledging that being a werewolf is just a part of you, go to page 177.

Approximately half an hour later, Java returns.

'Knock, knock,' he caws.

'Java! We don't have time for this!' Celeste snaps.

'Knock, knock,' he repeats.

Celeste sighs. 'Who's there?'

'Aren.'

'Aren who?'

'Aren't you excited to hear some more jokes?'

'Java! Where do we need to go?'

'Aw, you're no fun,' he says. 'The warlock's hut is on the north-east side of the mountain. I can show you.'

Michael jumps to his feet. 'OK, everyone ready?'

'I'm not going,' Katrina says.

Michael shoots her a nasty look.

She answers, 'I don't do heights, OK?'

'Well, you're going to have to get over it, aren't you?' Michael growls. 'Suck it up and get over it!'

'You are not in charge!' she shouts back, her voice breaking as a few tears run down her blushing face.

Michael turns to you. 'OK, captain. What should we do, then?'

The word 'fraud' flashes in your brain again. You have no idea how to handle the situation. Your shoulders tense and your hands feel cold and clammy. Then you take a breath.

'Katrina,' you say. 'We don't know what's out there. I sympathise with being uncomfortable with heights, but it would be helpful to have you and the dragopurrs with us, and I don't like

185

leaving you here alone while the rest of us go. I think it would be safer for us all if we stick together.'

'Fine!' she snaps and stands up. Her cheeks are no longer blushing. Instead, they are pale.

The journey up the mountain is slow and difficult. The road leading up to the mountain is not paved well, and only one slip, one misstep, can send you down, down, down. Michael and Celeste are in the lead again, trying to take the safest route. You follow their footsteps while remaining close to Katrina, whose breathing is getting heavier by the minute. Her face is entirely white now and she is shaking. Her anxiety seems so familiar that your own adrenaline almost seems to respond in turn.

'You OK?' you ask.

She drops to her knees, gasping for breath. 'I . . . can't . . . I'm . . . sorry.'

She looks down, screams and grabs the grass and earth on the ground, as if desperately trying to embrace it. Her lips are white and dry, and she trembles and shakes. The dragopurrs apparently sense her anguish because they take a seat on each side of her. Their enormous heads nuzzle at her legs as they purr.

'What's the holdup?' Michael demands.

'Give us a minute!' you snap back, feeling suddenly protective of Katrina, whose eyes look nearly as wide as her face. You kneel next to her and take her hand. 'What do you need?'

'I need to stay,' she replies weakly. 'I'm so sorry. I'm just not ready.' Tears are falling down her face.

Hera softly head-butts Katrina, affectionately rubbing her big furry face against Katrina's, wiping away her tears and purring loudly.

'OK,' you say, noticing Katrina's immediate look of relief. 'Can you get back down on your own?'

'Yes.' She nods.

'OK. Take the dragopurrs. When you're down there, work on training them.'

'Of course! I will. Thank you,' she says, smiling despite her tears.

You run to catch up with the rest of the group.

'She wimped out, eh?' Michael smirks.

'Leave her alone,' you respond in a firm voice.

Michael murmurs something under his breath but the rest of the journey is walked in silence, with the exception of an occasional directive from Java as he orients everyone from Celeste's left shoulder.

Suddenly, an eerie feeling comes over you. Something in your gut feels . . . numb. Your stomach feel empty but you are not hungry. Your entire body feels heavy, almost as if a part of you died. You no longer feel fear or insecurity. You feel nothing at all.

Endless.

Purposeless.

Empty.

It feels . . . grey.

In fact, the world around you becomes grey. The green mountain is now a dull, bald, grey road. You look around you. Everyone in your group is bewildered as well. Lex's green cardigan is now an amalgamation of several shades of grey. Everyone's skin is ashen. The fire in their eyes has gone out.

'What is this?' Lex asks.

'I don't know,' you respond.

'Ve need to find ze varlock as soon as possible,' Anka says in a worried voice.

You follow Java up a crooked hill until you arrive at a small and strange-looking cottage. It appears barely large enough to fit Lex. The cottage, like its surroundings, is grey and decorated by one window with wooden shutters. It is standing on two enormous chicken legs on the edge of a creepy swamp. Looking more closely at the swamp, you see that it's full of scattered bones from strange creatures. Here and there in the water and grass, sets of tiny eyes watch you.

The cottage has no door and you wonder how to get in when suddenly the chicken legs come to life. The house rises and turns 180 degrees on its legs, and now a door faces you and the legion. Moments later, the door opens.

You exchange glances with the others, your heart starting to pound again in your chest.

'Let's go,' Michael says and walks inside.

If you choose to follow him inside, go to page 55.

If you choose to wait outside and see what happens, go to page 56.

'OK,' you say after taking a long, settling breath, noticing that the Strah have surrounded you and each of your friends. 'If the Strah want me to give up, I will need to do the opposite.'

'*GIVE UP. WHY BOTHER? YOU ARE JUST GOING TO FAIL,*' the Strah threaten you again.

'Why bother?' you ask the swarm of Strah surrounding you. 'Because I care about the people Here. And even though I'm afraid, I am going to do the right thing anyway.'

The swarm surrounding you dissipates. The next biggest swarm is surrounding Talia. You run toward her, as do Gherk and Lex, who are also fighting off swarms of their own. Talia is on her knees, covering her face and crying. The Strah are swarming over her, feeding her their disgusting lies.

'*YOU ARE WEAK! YOU ARE BROKEN! NO ONE CAN PUT YOU BACK TOGETHER!*'

You pick up her face with your hands. 'Talia! Talia. Look at me! You are not your experiences. You are not broken. You are not weak. You are not a victim. You are a survivor. You are a vampire. You are our friend. Remember who you are, Talia.'

She looks up at you, her mascara smudged under her eyes. She takes a breath and stands.

'You are right,' she says, turning to face the Strah. 'I am not a victim. I am a survivor. I am not broken. I am not what happened to me. I am *me*.'

Some of the Strah around her dissipate, while the rest continue to torture her. '*YOU ARE FAT! AND IF YOU ARE FAT, THEN NOBODY*

190

*WILL EVER LOVE YOU. LEX WILL GROW SICK OF YOU. YOU
NEED TO LOSE WEIGHT AND YOU CAN NEVER EAT AGAIN.'*

'You know what?' Talia fires back. 'I can eat and I will.' She
takes out several vials from her purse. 'Oh. All empty. No matter.
Hey, Gherk! Can you please make me a blood cake?'

Gherk looks at her, astounded, as the swarm of Strah around
him grows larger.

*'YOU ARE SUCH A LOSER! YOU CANNOT EVER COOK
WITHOUT MESSING IT UP. YOUR OCD WON'T EVER LET
YOU BE NORMAL. YOU ARE A FREAK. AND IT IS YOUR
FAULT THAT YOUR WIFE LEFT YOU.'*

'Shut up!' Gherk yells at the Strah, who are temporarily taken
aback by his assertion and quiet down for a few moments. 'Good.
Now, uh, I am, uh, going to, uh, make a, uh, cake for, uh, my friend.'

He digs in his enormous apron and takes out several cookbooks.
Among them: *Cooking for Witches, Vegetarian and Human-Free
Cooking for Ogres* and *Vampire Favourites*. He puts the first two books
back in his apron and flips through the pages of the *Vampire Favourites*
until he finds the 'Best Blood Cake' recipe. He then takes out a crystal
bowl, a measuring cup, a bottle labelled 'Fresh Blood, O+', and other
ingredients that you cannot fully make out. He then takes out a sink
from his apron and rinses the bowl and the measuring cup.

The Strah appear to have now regained their courage because
they start their taunts again. *'YOU DID NOT CLEAN IT
ENOUGH. YOU NEED TO WASH THEM AGAIN.'*

Gherk turns the water back on.

'No, Gherk!' you shout over the Strah. 'Don't give in to your
fears! Remember that this is for Talia! This is for all of us!'

Gherk nods and turns off the water again. Then he walks back
toward Talia.

'THE BOWL ISN'T CLEAN! YOU ARE GOING TO KILL HER!'
Gherk growls but does not respond.

*'YOU SHOULD CHECK AT LEAST ONE MORE TIME TO
MAKE SURE IT'S REALLY CLEAN. IT WON'T TAKE LONG.
JUST DO IT. JUST CHECK.'*

Gherk sighs and rolls up his sleeve. He looks at his left arm, concentrating on his MESS mark, which reads: *You are HERE.* He then puts his hands on his heart.

'This is, uh, one of the, uh, hardest things I, uh, ever had to, uh, do. But, uh, this is, uh, for my friend.'

And with that, Gherk mixes all the ingredients, whisking in the heavy cream, the blood and the spices.

Seeing that the ogre is not easily manipulated, the Strah turn to Talia again. *'YOU ARE ACTUALLY GOING TO EAT THAT? THERE ARE SO MANY CALORIES IN THAT.'*

'Watch me,' she says as she scoops out a handful of cake batter with her bare hands.

'Remember about mindful eating,' you remind her.

'Thanks.' She smiles.

As the Strah are shouting their outrageous insults and fire up their scare tactics at her, Talia uses her senses to see the cake in her hands and to feel its sticky sensations on her fingers. She smells the dessert and then slowly puts a small piece of cake in her mouth, visibly savouring every bite. She smiles as she chews.

The remaining Strah near her try one more attempt. *'YOUR STOMACH IS SO FAT THAT YOU LOOK LIKE YOU ARE PREGNANT. YOU ARE DISGUSTING.'*

Talia stops eating. Her eyes fill up with tears. More Strah appear around her, apparently triggered by the shame and insecurity she is undoubtedly experiencing now.

'Fine,' she says quietly. 'You win.'

'No!' says Lex, approaching Talia. Lex kneels down in front of the vampire and softly kisses her stomach. 'You are so beautiful. And your stomach is beautiful.'

Talia looks at her partner and smiles. 'Thank you. I needed that.' She then turns toward the Strah and lifts up her shirt, exposing her stomach. 'Look. This is my stomach. I am not ashamed of it. I have hit it and mistreated it, but I will not hate it any more.'

As Lex, Talia and Gherk burst into tears, nearly half of the Strah are obliterated.

'You were right,' Lex says, sniffling. 'Facing your fears helps make the Strah less overwhelming.'

You smile at the elf and then turn to see who else needs your help. Over in the corner, Celeste is surrounded by a flock of Strah. She is pale and her eyes are full of terror. You run over to her. Your head throbs as you get nearer.

'Celeste, are you OK?'

She looks up at you, her eyes red and damp. Your own temples pulsate. You feel the enormous pressure around your eyes, the room starting to spin. You're nauseated from the overwhelming noise and light.

The Strah are ruthless with Celeste. *'YOU ARE NO HEALER. HOW CAN YOU HEAL ANYONE WHEN YOU CANNOT EVEN HEAL YOURSELF? HOW CAN YOU CALL YOURSELF A HEALER WHEN YOU COULDN'T SAVE JAVA? OR ANKA! OR BLAKE!'*

Celeste trembles and you feel a heavy hurt, grief and shame in your stomach, heart and throat.

Eribelle wakes up and runs over to you and Celeste.

'Oh, great! The Strah! What do we need to do?' Eribelle asks you. 'Does Celeste need to connect with her core values and heal someone?'

'Yes,' you say. 'Herself.'

Eribelle places Celeste's hands on the witch's heart. She then places her own fairy hands over Celeste's and says, 'Take a breath. Notice your own pain . . .'

Celeste follows her instructions, visibly calmer, tears running down her face as she breathes in and out.

Eribelle speaks softly but with intention. 'Many people want to protect others. Losing the people we care about hurts us all and we might all feel responsible, even though we are not. You always look out for everyone else but you deserve love and compassion too.'

Celeste sniffles as Eribelle continues. 'May you know how much you help others. May you know how loved you are. May you know how much you matter and how much of a difference you make.'

Celeste bursts into a sob and embraces Eribelle in a tight hug. As her breathing and tears slow down, the Strah around the two of them vanish.

The remaining Strah are split between Hoffman, Michael and Lex. Hoffman seems to have the largest swarm, so you run toward him, as Celeste and Talia run to help Lex, and Gherk, Eribelle and Katrina run to help Michael.

Hoffman looks pale when you reach him. He is breathing heavily, the Strah around him hissing ruthlessly, *'YOU ARE A COWARD! YOU ARE A FAILURE! YOU ARE FAILING YOUR JOB AND YOU ARE FAILING YOUR WIFE. YOU CAN'T SAVE HER. YOU CAN'T HELP HER. YOU ARE A FAILURE OF A HUSBAND. SHE TRUSTED YOU! SHE WILL DIE AND IT WILL BE ALL YOUR FAULT.'*

'Please. Please, what do I do?' he pleads with you, his voice breaking, and you can sense his heartache.

'Call her,' you say.

'Right now?'

'Yes. Tell her that you're coming home.'

'Uh . . . OK.'

He dials the number, trying to pay no attention to the hissing Strah. 'Hello? . . . Hi, honey . . . Yes . . . I know, sweetie . . . I miss you too . . . Take you to your infusion appointment?' He looks at you for guidance.

You nod.

He continues, 'Yes . . . I'll be there . . . Yes, I promise . . . I love you too . . .'

He kisses the phone and hangs up, then looks at you, his lower lip quivering, tears running down his cheeks. You feel the devastation in his heart. And you also feel his strength to face it all. The Strah around him seem to have sensed the same because they disappear. You give Hoffman a pat on the shoulder and run toward Michael.

'YOU ARE A COWARD! YOU ARE ALWAYS AFRAID TO TELL OTHERS HOW YOU FEEL ABOUT THEM. IF YOU TRUST SOMEONE, THEY WILL BETRAY YOU.'

'What should he do?' Eribelle looks at you.

You scratch your head. 'I'm actually not sure.'

'I think I know,' Michael says. Then he walks up to Katrina and takes her hands in his. 'Katrina, I think that you are the most wonderful and incredible woman I have ever met. You are courageous, compassionate and caring. The more I get to know you, the more I fall in love with you. You were the first one of all of us to face your fears. I know I have been a jerk. Please know that I love and respect you. And no matter what, I will always back your play.'

The Strah around him vanish as Michael and Katrina wipe away each other's tears and share a soft kiss. You call out to them and fill them in on your plan, before running over to Lex.

The remainder of the Strah circle around the elf, their ruthless remarks at the ready. *'YOUR PARENTS WERE ASHAMED OF YOU. THEY NEVER ACCEPTED YOUR SEXUAL IDENTITY. THEY NEVER ACCEPTED YOU. YOUR ONLY FRIEND WAS YOUR GUITAR. AND YOU WEREN'T EVEN GOOD AT IT! SHAME! YOU HAVE BROUGHT SHAME TO YOUR FAMILY!'*

Lex seems on the verge of tears and you feel the elf's shame and hurt.

'I think you've got to play, Lex,' you say.

Lex takes out the guitar but can't seem to start playing. Talia grabs Lex's hands. 'I believe in you,' she says.

'Thanks.' Lex smiles.

'Here,' Hoffman says. 'Let me help.'

He takes out a harmonica from his pocket. 'How about "Midnight Rain" by Two Owls and a Sparrow?'

'Sure.' Lex smiles again.

Hoffman presses his lips to the harmonica and begins to play. Lex looks embarrassed but joins him, as the elf sings:

> *Oh, it's raining again on my windowsill*
> *The drops softly hitting the glass*
> *And I know that the water will wash away*
> *And today's pain will all pass.*

As I sit here and judge myself
On the countless mistakes I have made
I work on self-compassion and I realise
This pain will fade, fade away.

And for now I will simply sit right Here
Listening to midnight rain,
And reflect that this moment is difficult
But I can cope with this pain.

The last of the Strah disappear as the elf continues to sing. Mallena watches with crossed arms and tightly pressed lips, so focused on the singing that she does not notice Katrina flying on Hera above her, with Hektor flying closely behind.

Suddenly, the dragopurrs take a sharp dive and knock the sorceress off her feet, tackling her to the ground. All of you rush over to help as Michael holds Mallena's hands behind her back. He takes out a pair of small pink gloves from his pocket and puts them on Mallena's hands. She attempts to cast a spell to free herself but the gloves seem to be inhibiting her ability to use magic.

'Picked them up when we were being taken away,' Michael explains.

Hoffman cuffs Mallena's gloved hands behind her back and helps her to sit in a chair.

'Let me go!' Mallena hisses. 'How *dare* you restrain me in my own castle?'

'We need to get the choker off her!' you shout. 'She's too emotionally numb to know what she's doing.'

'No!' Mallena shouts, and then her voice and facial expressions change as she now pleads. 'Please. Please! I don't want ... I can't ... Please don't remove it.'

'It's going to be OK,' you tell her, and then turn to Michael. 'Michael, I need your jacket.'

He takes it off and hands it to you without question. 'The Strah said I couldn't trust anyone. This'll show them.'

'Thank you,' you say, smiling. Then you gently place the jacket around Mallena, who is shaking her head. *Warmth, soft touch and soothing words,* you remind yourself. You kneel in front of her, placing your hands on her shoulders. 'I'm so sorry, Mallena. I know that you are scared. I know you're in pain . . .' You almost pass out from the sudden surge of pain you feel. You feel it all. The mind-blowing, devastating, excruciating pain of the entire world cumulated in your heart. You can hardly breathe. You close your eyes. Your heart is pounding, breaking, shattering.

'I vould have probably opted for ze choker too if I had to feel zis much pain every day,' a familiar voice says.

'Anka?' You open your eyes and see that you are no longer in the cold grey library, you are now in a bright, beautiful garden, sitting next to a family of hedgehogs. Anka is holding one of them as she sits next to you.

'Oh, no. Am I dead?' you ask, and then mentally kick yourself, realising that this is probably not the most thoughtful thing to ask a recently deceased person.

Anka, however, does not seem to be offended. She smiles at you as she pets the hedgehog in her lap. 'No. You are not dead. You vere in pain. Your heart vas hurting. Just like Mallena's vas some time ago.'

'I don't understand. What does me being able to understand Mallena's pain have to do with anything? A lot of people are empathic. Why am I different? Most of the time I am too much of a mess to help anyone.'

'Yes.' She smiles. 'You are MESS. You are MESS because you are empat. It is true zat many people feel empasy, but only true empats can feel ze pain and suffering of ozers ze vay zat empats can. Zis is vhy empats are often more likely to have depression or anxiety. But understand zis: empasy is very special super power. Ze very sing zat most people sink of as veakness, is actually your greatest strengs.'

You have about a thousand more questions for her, but all you can get out is, 'Umm . . .'

Therapy Quest

'It is time for me to go. But remember zat if you ever need me, I vill alvays be right Here.' With those words fading in your ears, she vanishes and you find yourself back at the library.

You are kneeling in front of Mallena, her face pale, her eyes wide with fear, her lips trembling. 'Mallena. I'm only now beginning to understand the pain that you've endured when you felt the suffering of everyone Here. It's excruciating. Anyone in your situation would want to run away and not feel it. I understand how much it hurts to see the people you care about suffer, and the impulse to avoid it at all costs. However, the choker doesn't take the pain away. Not really. It only masks it while poisoning you, making the very essence of your being disappear.'

Mallena whimpers, her breathing now more shallow, as you continue. 'I know that you were hoping to take away the suffering of others but the truth is that we cannot selectively mute certain emotions. It tends to be an all-or-none deal. The choker took away your empathic distress, your depression, your heartbreak, but it also muted your ability to experience joy, happiness and hope. It took away your ability for compassion and humanity.'

She shudders, a single tear rolling down her cheek. You feel her heart warming as you begin the Loving Kindness practice of the Moon Tradition.

'Mallena, I have some wishes for you, from my heart to yours. May you be happy. May you be free from pain and suffering.'

She sniffles as you continue. 'May you know how loved you are. May you know how much you matter.'

Mallena looks into your eyes and repeats, 'May you know how loved you are. May you know how much you matter.'

CRACK!

The choker splits, shattering into several fragile pieces that lose their sparkle to the shadows on the dark floor.

Proceed to page 28.

MaineHealth
Learning Resource Center

Item number: _17821_

Title: _Therapy Quest_

First Name: _____

Last Name: _____

Address: _____

City: _____

State: